# KNITWEAR DESIGN

**LAURENCE KING**

Published in 2013 by
Laurence King Publishing Ltd
361–373 City Road
London EC1V 1LR
Tel: +44 20 7841 6900
Fax: +44 20 7841 6910
e-mail: enquiries@laurenceking.com
www.laurenceking.com

ISBN: 978 1 78067 058 4
A catalogue record for this book is
available from the British Library.

Design by Eleanor Ridsdale Design
Senior editor: Peter Jones

Printed in China.

MIX
Paper from
responsible sources
FSC® C104723

LAURENCE KING PUBLISHING

# KNITWEAR DESIGN

## CAROL BROWN

# CONTENTS:

# INTRODUCTION

In recent years knitting has seen a resurgence in popularity, with many different approaches emerging – from creative international catwalk fashions through to the application of knitting in interiors in the form of lightshades, cushions, floor coverings, chairs and blinds, all based on the versatility of stitch structure. Conceptual artists, too, have exploited the traditional craft of knitting to create installations of all dimensions, from large-scale public sculptures to miniatures and wearable art, all of which challenge our preconceptions of knitting.

Knitting's increased popularity has been assisted and promoted by the internet and the growth of a virtual community of knitters who subscribe to the many popular and well-established websites, online journals and magazines. There are many internet bloggers and photo bloggers who regularly show images of their work, provide links to other web pages and are active in encouraging readers to become involved in discussion forums.

**Above:** 'How My Mother Dressed Me' by Karen Searle, hand knitting and copper wire. Each dress measures 17.8cm high.

**Below:** 'Ktog (Knit Together)' installation by Rania Hassan, worked in oil, fibre, canvas, metal and wood.

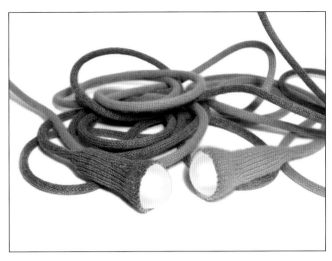

**Above:** Concepts in interior lighting – flexible knitted 'Matt lights' produced in strong mercerised cotton by Ilot Ilov, a company founded in 2006, located in Kreuzberg, Berlin.

**Left:** 'Form and Function' by Claire-Ann O'Brien, commissioned by Rowan Wool, original seating exploring new applications for knitting in product and interior design.

**Below:** PHAT KNITS is a series of giant threads used to create knitted and sculptural interior products by Dutch designer Bauke Knottnerus. They were exhibited at the Momu Fashion Museum in Antwerp, the Netherlands, in 2011.

Fibre Fest 2011 community knitting installation 'Above and Below the Waves', inspired by the Devonshire coastline, supported by Arts Council funding and led by textile artist Alison Murray with 2,000-plus knitters.

Another current trend is the growing interest in knitting as a community activity. Groups meet regularly in churches, cafés and on the street to sit, knit and chat, sharing ideas and swapping patterns. Some groups meet to socialize, learn and develop new skills, while others knit for charity, for therapy or to 'knit' for social change. Knitting and activism – known as 'knit bombing' or 'graffiti knitting' – has become widespread globally, with activist groups expressing their concern for the environment and other social and political causes by creating knitted installations and 'knit bombing' the environment.

These groups have been reinforced by knit-ins, knitting retreats and knitting festivals such as Unravel and Knit Nation, both in the UK. The knitting festivals feature highly organized event programmes of exhibitions, live demonstrations and workshops, with the opportunity to purchase yarns, equipment and knitting merchandise from exhibiting stalls.

The largest community event to date is the annual World Wide Knit in Public Day, established in 2005 by Danielle Landes. In its first year it comprised more than 25 events staged around the world. Each year this event has continued to attract greater interest and recognition and now involves over 800 events. It encourages knitting groups across the globe to interact with each other, attracting a generation of new young knitters. It also results in many collaborative knitting projects, with large-scale public installations and interdisciplinary projects between artists and craft workers developing within and between groups.

This revival of knitting in the twenty-first century has transformed our view of the craft. This book explores knitting by discussing the techniques, traditions and contemporary concepts in fashion that have resulted in a profusion of exciting contemporary designs and developments. It examines new ideas and developments in the field of knitted textiles and design, featuring the work of some of the most exciting international designers in knitwear today.

Whether you are a student, designer, practitioner or home knitter you will find this book a source of inspiration – illustrated throughout with samples, diagrams and garment designs, demonstrating the potential of knitting and offering a wealth of techniques that can be explored and adapted for both hand and machine knitting.

**Top:** 'World Wide Knit in Public Day' – the largest knitting event in the world, started in 2005 by Danielle Landes, encouraged knitters to join in community knitting events across the globe to celebrate the craft of knitting and fibre arts.

**Above:** 'Knit Knot Tree', Yellow Springs, Ohio; yarn-bombed tree by the Jafagirls.

**Right:** 'Elaine's Bench' in Yellow Springs, Ohio, a colourful patchwork of knit and crochet tagged by the Jafagirls who have been yarn bombing since 2007.

# 1
# THE KNITTING
# INDUSTRY

The practice of knitting, whether applying traditional techniques or new technology, covers a huge field and a vast array of techniques and processes, from hand knitting through to seamless knitting technology. This chapter discusses the manufacturing, design and sampling methods within the fashion knitting industry. It also profiles the range of career opportunities available in the industry and, finally, explores the international trade exhibitions that provide a space for a range of exhibitors – from spinners to designers – to display knitted textiles and manufacturing machinery.

**Top left:** Lady's 1930s knitted short-sleeved jumper with decorative patterned yoke and fluted sleeve detailing by Patons and Baldwins', a leading UK manufacturer of yarn and knitting publications.

**Bottom left:** Patons and Baldwins' Lady's 1930s bathing suit from 'Diana' non-shrink 4 ply knitting wool.

**Top right:** Patons and Baldwins' Lady's 1930s bathing suit from 'Crocus' non-shrink 4 ply knitting wool, giving full pattern instructions stating, 'As woollen fabric expands a little when wet, a Swimming Suit must fit the figure firmly before it is worn in water, otherwise it will be liable to sag'.

**Bottom right:** Lady's vintage 1930s knitted jumper with short tulip sleeves with gathered detailing in 2 ply yarn from Patons and Baldwins'.

PATONS & BALDWINS' HELPS TO KNITTERS 3/559

PRICE 3D.

## LADY'S JUMPER
FROM PATON'S SUPER OR BEEHIVE FINGERING

## LADY'S BATHING SUIT
FROM "CROCUS" NON-SHRINK KNITTING

N° 3716 PATONS & BALDWINS' HELPS TO KNITTERS PRICE 3D.

## LADY'S BATHING SUIT
FROM "DIANA" NON-SHRINK KNITTING

N° 3749 PATONS & BALDWINS' HELPS TO KNITTERS PRICE 3D.

PATONS & BALDWINS' HELPS TO KNITTERS 3/620

PRICE 3D.

## LADY'S JUMPER
FROM PATON'S SUPER, OR BEEHIVE, FINGERING

Crossover tunic design with intricate sleeve and shoulder detailing by Coven in dark green, black and charcoal grey with stunning gold highlights, shown at Fashion Rio, Rio De Janeiro, Brazil, Autumn/Winter 2010.

# WEFT AND WARP KNITTING TECHNIQUES

There are two main forms of knitting: weft and warp knitting. Weft-knitted fabrics consist of a continuous looped structure of interlocking stitches or courses extending horizontally, and can be knitted with one continuous length of yarn. This creates fabrics suitable for fashion garments. The structure, however, means that work can easily be unravelled. Weft-knitted fabrics are the most common form of knitting and can be produced by hand using knitting needles, or produced on a domestic or industrial knitting machine.

Warp knitting is formed from loops of yarn zigzagging and linking in a vertical direction, creating very stable fabrics that cannot be unravelled. Warp-knitted fabric is produced by machine using one warp yarn for each wale; the wale is the vertical line of loops in knitting that each stitch hangs from. Warp-knitted fabric is used for corsetry, underwear, lingerie, sports fabrics, nets and tulle, curtaining and trims.

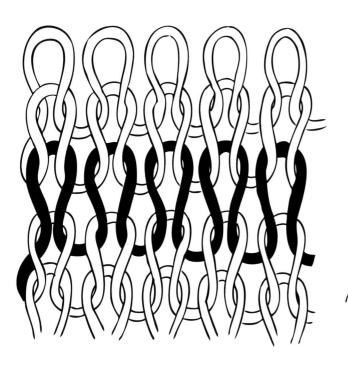

Weft-knitted farbric

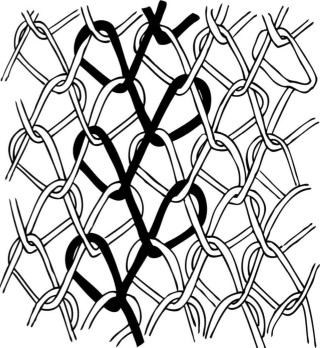

Warp-knitted fabric

# HAND VS MACHINE KNITTING

Garments can be produced by hand knitting using two or more needles, a technique that is relatively slow compared to knitting by machine. There is, however, a fantastic array of yarns available specifically for the hand-knitting market, and the hand knitter also has the advantage of full control over the growth of the design, manipulating every stitch by hand. Hand knitting in fashion design became very popular in the 1970s and 80s, with the development of artisan hand knits inspired by the colourful work of the textile artist Kaffe Fassett, who brought knitting to the masses through the publication of books, including *Glorious Knits*, and the broadcast of his knitting series on television. At this time, too, knitwear started to gain recognition in the fashion world, as designers began including it in their collections and knitwear labels hit the catwalk. A surge of knitters, including Sandy Black, Susan Duckworth, Marion Foale, Sasha Kagan and Patricia Roberts launched designs under their own names and labels. This growth in the presence of knitting on the catwalk was mirrored in the knitting-pattern market. Knitting patterns had previously been mass-produced and churned out by yarn spinners who paid very little attention to fashion. Now designer books of knitting patterns started to appear, launched with their own designer yarn ranges – a trend that continues today.

In the 1970s and 80s machine knitting was also becoming popular among the general public, with the publication of many new magazine titles, including *Machine Knitting News* and *Machine Knitting Monthly* in the UK and the American *Machine Knitting Source* by Fiber Circle Publications. These magazines promoted domestic machine knitting, providing features on machine-knitting techniques, readers' ideas, knitwear patterns and the latest in domestic machine technology. Hand and machine knitting have both survived; however, in recent years it is the hand-knitting market that has really developed in its appeal to the home knitter, as a result of the development of new yarns, the creativity and the portability of hand knitting, the promotion of the craft by celebrities, the collaborative projects that have developed between art disciplines, and the community knitting groups that have sprung up globally. The domestic-machine knitting market, by contrast, became over-saturated with magazines, the launch of new machines, accessories and yarns, and it has not held up as well as the more socially adaptable craft of hand knitting. Knitwear has, however, held its place in fashion due to the extraordinary growth of new young designers specializing in knit, including Julien Macdonald, Mark Fast, Sandra Backlund, Claire Tough and Derek Lawlor – all names synonymous with success.

Figure-hugging blue dress in a range of knitted textures with gilt-chain detailing by Claire Tough.

# KNIT CONSTRUCTION

There are two main methods of knitwear construction: fully fashioned and cut and sew. Due to advances in machine knit technology and the introduction of seamless garments, however, these categories are becoming blurred.

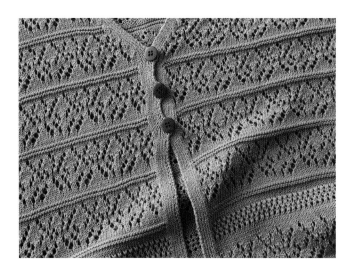

**Left and below:** Highly textured 'birch grey' cable sleeveless top knitted using the WHOLEGARMENT/Shima Seiki system that allows many different stitch combinations in various gauges to be knitted in a garment.

**Above:** Fully fashioned knitwear

## FULLY FASHIONED KNITWEAR

Fully fashioned knitwear is produced by knitting each garment component exactly to the shape required for each pattern piece, by increasing and decreasing the number of stitches and shaping the piece by stitch transfer to the calculated measurements of the garment design. The production time is lengthy because the garments are usually made up by joining the seams together using a linking technique that gives a neat professional finish, and also by applying finishing processes to give a perfect, comfortable fit. This method of manufacturing is generally used for knitwear that is produced in luxurious fibres, such as cashmere, lambswool, vicuna, merino, silk and linen, producing knit fabrics for the higher end of the market.

In recent years the iconic brand, Pringle of Scotland, which was founded in 1815, has been involved in many collaborative projects, taking its traditional heritage and mixing it with contemporary design and new technology. The brand has been developed and launched into the international luxury fashion arena by showing at both London and Milan Fashion Weeks. It has also linked up with many famous Scottish names, such as the award-winning actress Tilda Swinton and the artists Jim Lambie and Alasdair Gray, to give the brand real gravitas as a label of quality and distinction by playing on its Scottish heritage and strong design appeal.

Fine Dubied pleated Lurex and acrylic knit dress Spring/Summer 2011 collection 'Fossil Warriors' by Alice Palmer.

Turquoise fully fashioned, '60s-inspired knitted dress by heritage knitwear label Pringle of Scotland.

Fully fashioned fine-gauge intarsia colour-blocked knitted sweater worn with grey flannel trousers by Pringle of Scotland – Spring/Summer 2012 collection, presenting a new take on the iconic Argyle styling, for which Pringle are renowned.

**Top left:** A very feminine style with sculptured, open-work detailing forming the garment yoke by Danish designer Iben Høj.

**Bottom left:** Detail of fine gauge crêpe knit using partial knitting technique to add shaping, fullness and flare to the bodice top by Iben Høj.

**Top right:** Iben Høj is renowned for her technical understanding of stitch structure, as illustrated in the delicate detailing of this knitted garment using partial knitting techniques.

**Bottom right:** Delicate white, fine-gauge top using partial knitting technique to add shape, flare and drape to the silhouette by Iben Høj.

## CUT AND SEW

The cut-and-sew method is the simplest and cheapest way of constructing knitwear produced commercially. To make the lower price point of the end product financially viable and attractive, the manufacturing processes are much quicker, and the types of yarn used – acrylic blends, cotton and polyester mixes, acrylic wool and polyester combinations – produce fabrics that are machine washable and relatively easy to care for. The fabric is knitted on a V-bed or flatbed knitting machine, as described on page 22, or alternatively, tubular lengths of fabric can be made on a circular knitting machine. The lengths of fabric are knitted and then pressed. Layers of knitted fabric are stacked up on top of one another and the garment pieces are then cut out in bulk using automatic cutters, in a similar way to woven fabrics. The garments are then overlocked and the seams sewn together. Any garment components – for example, neck ribs, pockets and knit trims – are produced separately and attached during the finishing process.

**Above:** Colour-blocked jacquard knits by designer Ginna Lee, whose personal aim is to 'create abstract visual manifestations of specific emotional moments or states' through her work.

**Below:** Cut and sew. The fabric is knitted to the required length and width, the garment pieces are cut from the fabric, and then sewn together.

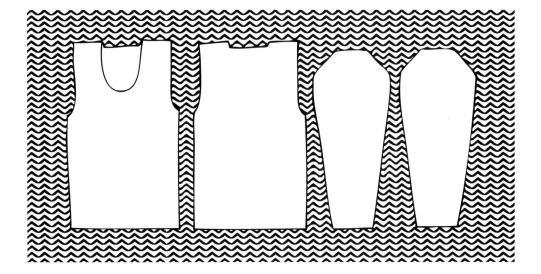

# SEAMLESS KNITTING

One of the most exciting technological advances in the knitting industry, introduced in 1995 at the International Textile Machinery Association (ITMA), is the development of innovative seamless knitting technology, which has resulted in the making of whole garments with 3D shaping. The production of seamless garments involves little or no cutting and sewing after production, saving time, labour and yarn costs. Seamless knitting has grown in popularity due to its wearability, combining a flattering fit and smooth shaping with the comfort factor of no seams, and has been adopted by the underwear, sportswear, activewear and knitwear markets.

Many designers have adopted seamless knitting technology. Cutting-edge designer Issey Miyake's 'A-POC' custom collection was started in 1997 in collaboration with engineering designer Dai Fujiwara. It was 'founded in the philosophy of clothing made from "a Piece of Cloth", a concept which explores not only the relationship between the body and clothing, but also the space that is born between them.' The collection comprises tubes of machine-produced seamless fabric designed to be cut into various lengths and shapes, and customized by and to the consumer's individual design requirements.

**Below:** Knit installation 'Anyway', 2002, by textile artist Freddie Robins. A 1650 x 3000 x 3000mm series of large-scale, tubular, 'interconnected four-limbed sweaters' exploring seamless knitting technology.

**Above:** Fabrics are suspended from the ceiling exhibiting the inspirational Issey Miyake 'A-POC' (A Piece of Cloth) range developed by Dai Fujiwara. The concept began in 1997 and is revolutionary in that the engineering of the garments occurs while the fabric is still on the roll.

# KNITTING MACHINES

There are many different types of knitting machine, from the simple domestic knitting machine to a wide range of industrial machines. Each machine has its own specialist capabilities.

Domestic knitting machines are the most popular machines for home knitters and small design studios. They are easy to operate and are available in fine, standard gauge and chunky gauge. The machine knitting gauge refers to the distance between the needles on the machine bed and also defines the thickness of yarns the machine can handle. A fine-gauge machine knits lightweight fabrics and a standard-gauge machine knits good sports-weight fabrics, while the chunky gauge is better suited to light, bulky yarns, hand-knit type yarns and more textured novelty yarns. Machines usually have an integrated punch-card mechanism or pattern stitch mechanism for programming pattern stitch repeats, such as Fair Isle (see page 89), tuck and lace patterning.

Domestic knitting machines have various attachments and additional carriages that are usually sold separately, including lace and intarsia carriages and yarn changer and ribber attachments. Domestic machines have a single bed of needles. If a ribber is added it forms two flat beds, which then creates a double-bed machine – the ribber can be used to knit the ribbing of a garment and then lowered to allow the main body of the garment to be knitted on a single bed, if required. A full garment can be produced on a single-bed machine; however, a double bed gives greater versatility, producing both plain and purl fabrics. The single bed produces knit stitches and the ribber knits the purl. A double bed allows for the production of an almost unlimited range of fabrics, including double-bed jacquard, circular tube fabrics and ribbed structures.

The domestic machine is useful for creating and developing new ideas, being easy to work on and excellent for hand manipulation techniques, such as cabling, decorative partial knitting, and decorative lace trims, edgings and fringing.

**Top:** Standard-gauge, domestic knitting machine with single bed .

**Below:** Dubied hand-flat industrial knitting machine, showing the 'V-bed', which is hand-operated, and is available in a variety of gauges producing very fine lightweight fabrics to chunky weight. Swedish School of Textiles in Boras.

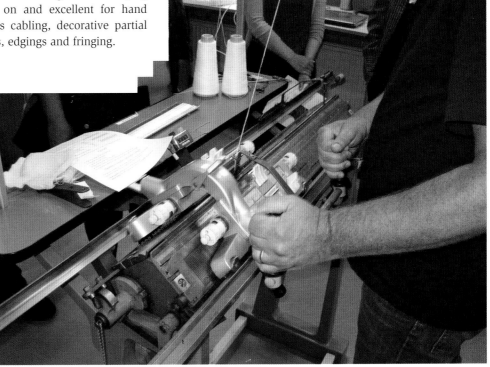

Industrial hand flats are hand-operated industrial knitting machines. The Dubied knitting machine, for example, is a hand flat manufactured by the Swiss company of the same name. The machine is no longer in production but it is still used by many independent designers and small businesses, due to the hand operation and the versatility of the machine's stitch capabilities. Small design studios often use these machines for producing fabric swatches, exploring colour, texture and knit techniques, and creating sample garments. Industrial hand flats are produced in a variety of gauges, ranging from around 16gg to 1.5gg, with 16gg being a very fine gauge, having 16 needles per inch, and 1.5gg being a chunky gauge. Industrial hand flats have a 'V-bed', consisting of two knitting beds that are angled and meet in an inverted 'V' structure that can produce a wide range of stitch structures, such as double-knit jacquards, ribbing and tubular fabrics.

Circular knitting machines are available in a wide range, from those that are powered mechanically or electronically to those that are controlled by computer. All produce lengths of seamless tubular fabric in various gauges, including single to double jerseys, jacquards, ribbed fabrics, fleece, mesh and double-faced fabrics for specific purposes, including hosiery, sports outerwear, and household and medical textiles.

Automatic, fully fashioned flat knitting machines are a development of the traditional flat knitting machine. They have an automatic fully fashioned function that is controlled by an imported computer and are relatively easy to programme and use. The fabric design is created on the computer software and the information is then fed directly to the electronic flatbed machine, which knits the design.

**Above:** Circular knitting machine producing three-colour jacquard fabric.

**Below:** Digital knitted fabrics produced in 50 per cent merino wool and 50 per cent Egyptian cotton. 'Only the best Italian yarns are selected for this collection. The colours are not seasonal, they are selected to create a special Emdal identity and balance.'

# COMPUTERIZED FLAT KNITTING MACHINES

Designers continually seek and explore new methods of production, investigating the potential of the machine and developing new technology. Computerized flat knitting machines are controlled by knitting technology software and can be used to design knit structures such as jacquard and intarsia patterns, as well as flat patterns. They also have flexible knitting speeds that can be adjusted. Quality and productivity are important factors in the fashion and textile industry, and the latest machines have been designed to achieve maximum efficiency without reducing standards. Advances in machine knitting have enhanced the capabilities of knitwear production, resulting in the introduction of seamless or whole garment knitting.

**Top right:** Knitted fabrics being designed digitally by Emdal for DANSK Autumn/Winter 2010/11 Fashion and Interior collection.

**Middle right:** Digital knitted fabrics designed and produced on an industrial knitting machine at Emdal ColorKnit factory.

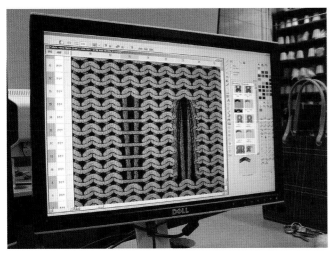

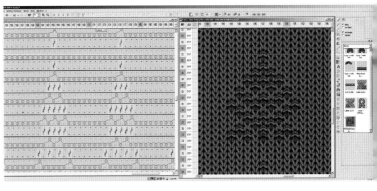

**Above:** CAD programs enable the designer to develop ideas for jacquards, intarsia patterning, placement motifs and other techniques. The screen image shown illustrates the difference between slip and tuck stitch.

**Left:** Digital hooded 'Tree' cape by Emdal ColorKnit, a company established by Danish textile designer and artist Signe Emdal.

# SEAMLESS KNITTING TECHNOLOGY

The two main suppliers of V-bed knitting machines are Shima Seiki in Japan and Stoll in Germany – two companies that work at the forefront of knit technology to develop products ranging from knit design software to standard computerized flat knitting machines and seamless knitting technology. Shima Seiki produces several different 'WHOLEGARMENT®' knitting systems, from very fine to coarse gauge. Stoll produces 'Knit and Wear®' garment technology using similar systems in a range of gauges, creating multi-gauge fabrics from fine to coarse, with the coarse gauge giving a hand-knitted appearance. Knitting-machine technology is constantly being refined and developed to improve performance and set-up times, increase production speeds and enable machines to knit a greater range of stitch structures.

In seamless garment production, the garment components – front, back and sleeves – are all knitted as tubes, with each component using a separate cone of yarn fed through separate yarn feeders at the same time. The shaping of the garment is worked by a computer program and then during the knitting process the components join, merging into one garment. This process results in the production of garments that are comfortable and, as Stoll describes, 'a perfect fit, providing new freedom in shape and design, high fabric quality and the elimination of bothersome seams'.

Stoll automatic knitting machine, which is able to produce 'knit and wear' garments at high productivity levels, in a wide range of knitted structures including intarsia patterning.

# THE FUTURE OF KNITTING TECHNOLOGY

There are many collaborative and interdisciplinary links between knit designers and artists, scientists and architects which stimulate ideas, resulting in new concepts and product developments. Research has been vital in the development of smart textiles, which have included medical textiles, light-emitting textiles and scan-to-knit technology – all of which have improved and advanced the development of knitted structures, and the performance of fabrics and production practices, which are discussed in further detail in Chapter 4 (see p.134).

'A Tree Tale' - Knitted installation exploring perspective and scale by Danish digital knit brand Emdal ColorKnit, who have a history of working in collaboration in the fields of fashion, textiles, home décor, set and costume design and art exhibitions.

Veronika Persché working in her Viennese knitting studio workshop producing fabrics for designers (fashion) and artists internationally.

CASE STUDY

# VERONIKA PERSCHÉ

Textile designer Veronika Persché was born in Klosterneuburg, Austria, and since 1999 has worked as a freelance designer, producing contemporary fabrics for international fashion designers and artists from her knit design studio in Vienna. Veronika trained in textile design, graduating from the College of Textile Design at the HTBLVA in Vienna. She is renowned for her exploration and fabric manipulation, resulting in innovative three-dimensional fabric structures that involve the techniques of tuck and jacquard, frequently produced using a computer-driven flatbed knitting machine. The techniques she applies to her work allow her to explore her love of colour, producing samples in a wide range of colourways. Yarns used in her work include viscose, which is renowned for its draping properties, and merino wool, cotton/viscose and wool/latex, all of which play an important role in developing the intricate three-dimensional surface structures for which she is recognized.

Veronika has worked on collaborative projects, exhibitions and freelance assignments with many artists and designers, including fashion labels Elfenkleid, Szidonia Szep, Elizaveta Fateeva and Eva Gronbach, and the jewellery designer Sonja Bischur. Her work has been shown at the International Trade Fair for the Skilled Trades in Munich and at several exhibitions, including 'Around 30' at Galerie Handwerk in Koblenz, 'Folge 02' in Vienna and 'Austrian Talents' at Galeria X in Bratislava. She has exhibited her ecological textiles at the Ethical Fashion Source Expo in London. She has guest lectured at the Academy of Fine Arts in Vienna, and led textile-design workshops at the Haute Ecole d'Art et de Design (HEAD) in Geneva. Her work is regularly reviewed in international magazines and journals, including *Selvedge*, *Textile Forum* and *Fibre Arts*.

**What type of formal training did you have?**
I attended a craft school and finished with an apprenticeship as a gold and pearl embroiderer. After that I completed a textile design programme at a college in Vienna.

**What inspires and influences your designs?**
I am strongly influenced by people (and what they are wearing), and by architecture and old buildings with their ornamented facades, so Vienna with its architecture and people from Eastern Europe is an amazing source of inspiration. I also enjoy travelling to gather new impressions of other places.

**Can you describe your design process in a few sentences?**
I collect images of ornamental detailing from a wide range of sources – plastered façades, decorative furniture, motifs I find on a headscarf. I then combine them to create new motifs. I convert these drawings into design files for my knitting machines. Most of my work is geometrical. The most amazing part of the process is when I try out the patterns on the machine, using and combining different techniques and materials; this is where the magic takes place. Very often I get the most beautiful and stunning surprises because of some accident!

**Left:** Close-up detailing of dramatic three-dimensional structured knit by Veronique Persché.

**Below:** Close-up detailing of three-dimensional knit produced by manipulating the fabric using a tucking technique, a form of 'on-machine gathering' produced on a computer driven flatbed knitting machine by Veronika Persché.

**What types of machine are used in the production of your work?**

I use three different models of computerized flatbed knitting machines.

**What techniques do you apply to your work?**

All kinds actually, but less so hand-manipulation techniques. I prefer using my machines in an 'industrial' way so, for example, I almost always use the motor.

**What is the most difficult part of designing a collection?**

The majority of my work involves freelance contracts and collaborating with fashion, costume and interior designers. I need a couple of weeks to get into the right mode to integrate all my ideas into new knitted fabric designs.

**Which international trade events do you show at?**

There are a few business-to-business events I attend where designers and manufacturers meet, such as Source Expo in London.

**What is the most challenging part of your job?**

The most challenging but also most satisfying part of my job is dealing with or pushing the boundaries of technical limitations. I like the moments when I have to concentrate on a solution to make a special design work on my knitting machines.

# CAREERS IN KNITWEAR

If you are interested in a career in the knitting industry, consider undertaking one of the many courses available both nationally and internationally. These range from highly technical programmes aimed at those interested in a career in textile technology and production development to courses aimed at training fabric and garment designers. Courses are available within colleges and universities. Short courses, specialized training sessions, conferences, seminars and workshops are also provided by machine manufacturers such as Stoll, who provide training covering a wide array of knitwear-related topics, from 'Quality assurance in knitwear production' to 'Best practices for developing technical spec sheets', among many others.

The fashion and textile industry is one of the largest industry sectors and knitted textiles play an important role. Areas of employment are wide-ranging; positions include: technical designer, product developer, yarn developer, knitwear consultant, pattern cutter, pattern grader and pattern writer for the hand-knitting market. Some job titles merge – for example, technician/machine programmer – so it is worth looking at the outline provided in a particular job description to appreciate the job criteria.

**Above:** A stunning presentation of fine-gauge fabrics at Pitti Filati.

**Left:** Fabric board by Emdal ColorKnit, a digital knit brand established by the Danish textile designer and artist Signe Emdal.

| PROFESSION | DESCRIPTION |
| --- | --- |
| KNITWEAR DESIGNER | There are many opportunities for designers within the knitwear industry, which include working for companies that supply wholesalers, independent outlets and high-street retailers. This may include fully fashioned, seamless or cut-and-sew knitwear, or the hand-knitting sector in womenswear, menswear, childrenswear or the accessory market. Companies range in size from large through medium-sized to the smaller companies and independent sole traders.

The role of a knitwear designer varies greatly, depending on the size of the company and the market level. Usually, however, a knitwear designer should have natural creative flair and be able to design and develop garment ranges to a customer's or client's brief. They should have a good eye for colour and texture, and be able to create sketches and mood boards showing seasonal ideas for product development, including detailed technical flats.

Jobs are advertised at all levels under many different titles, which include: senior knitwear designer, assistant and junior knitwear designer, and technical designer. The designer is usually required to work to a customer's brief, liaise and visit overseas suppliers, and create commercial on-trend ranges.

Often knit jobs are advertised in a particular market sector, such as women's/girls' jersey wear, women's circular knitwear or commercial men's knitwear. The advertisement and job description will provide an outline of what the position involves. Whatever the sector, a designer should have a good knowledge of various types and gauges of machine or an understanding of hand knitting capabilities, and must be able to develop sample ideas on hand flats or domestic knitting machines. They must have a good working knowledge of pattern cutting, garment construction and manufacturing techniques, fabric, yarns and trims, and be IT literate, with a working knowledge of CAD – for instance, Adobe Photoshop and Illustrator.

A knitwear designer should have good communication skills and be able to work and liaise with both internal and external departments, such as the design director, the product manager/developer, the pattern cutter and the production team, external suppliers, factories, buyers and clients. They must be able to present their range ideas within specific pricing/budgetary guidelines and be able to prepare presentation material for the team, company directors and in preparation for buying meetings.

Due to the pace of the industry and turnaround of garments and seasonal ranges, a designer must be able to work to targets and tight deadlines, meeting all the critical dates in managing the design process. |
| PATTERN CUTTER/ PATTERN GRADER/ PATTERN WRITER | The role of the pattern cutter is to draft the first pattern from the designer sketch or working drawing using in-house block patterns or alternatively by modelling on the stand, or draping – or by using a combination of both methods. They will be able to work from 2D to 3D and be able to fit and grade, alter and reconstruct patterns by hand or using CAD. Depending on the size of the company or studio, a pattern cutter will work in liaison with the designer and the production manager to perfect the sample garment, and then prepare it for production. |

| PROFESSION | DESCRIPTION |
| --- | --- |
| PRODUCT DEVELOPER | The product developer monitors all the production processes and procedures, including the management and coordination of suppliers in the sample development stages, and is involved with the quality inspection of the knit and the garment. A product developer needs to have an excellent knowledge of various types and gauges of machine, hand-knitting capabilities, knitting techniques, stitches, grading standards and the production technology for the manufacturing of the type of knitwear produced, such as cut and sew. They must be able to sort out technical problems, correct patterns and coordinate all knit programme details with buyers and suppliers while working and meeting all approval dates. |
| KNITTING MACHINE TECHNICIAN/ PROGRAMMER | Knitwear technicians are usually employed to programme industrial knitting machines using CAD systems, and also to sort out any problems and knitting faults. A knitting technician/programmer must have a full working knowledge of how to programme selected knitting machines to work to the most efficient production time. |
| MACHINE OPERATOR | Machine operators manage the machines and carry out overall maintenance and servicing, making sure machines are running efficiently and effectively. They maintain yarn supplies for knit runs during a machine's operation, as many machines will have several cones of yarn feeding in at any one time. |
| FABRIC TECHNOLOGIST | Fabric technologists are responsible for matters relating to fibre, yarn and fabric structure, aesthetics and performance. The fabric technologist is involved in the development of new and innovative fabrics based on seasonal trends and clients' requirements. The technologist must have a thorough knowledge of knitting machines, as they are responsible for maintaining and controlling the quality systems in the production of yarns and fabrics, ensuring that the knitted fabric meets the customer's specifications within the target budget. They will check the quality systems in the mills during production and suggest improvements when and where possible. |
| KNITWEAR GARMENT TECHNOLOGIST | A knitwear garment technologist needs an excellent understanding of manufacturing, construction processes, garment assembly and the sampling process, which involves controlling production and quality standards. Responsibilities include working in close liaison with the designer and production team to work out the size specifications and the planning out of how garments are to be made up, making any necessary changes to improve their quality and standard. |
| YARN DEVELOPER/ SPINNER AND COLOURIST | Yarn developers, spinners and colourists are often employed by spinning companies or trend forecasting agencies. They need an excellent understanding of colour combinations, fibres, how to blend yarns, yarn types, finishes, new developments and an awareness of forthcoming trends. |
| KNITWEAR CONSULTANT | Many knitwear consultancies offer a full range of knitwear-related services to the fashion and textile industries, working with individual clients, from yarn spinners to knitwear manufacturers. Their services usually include colour prediction, yarn, fabric, colour and swatch development, garment design, production and technical support. Other opportunities are also available in the specialist areas of accessory design, product and interiors, for example producing knitted fabrics for blinds, throws, cushions and soft furnishings, or designing knitted fabrics for industrial interiors. |

| PROFESSION | DESCRIPTION |
| --- | --- |
| KNIT AGENT | Many knit designers who establish their own business or work as freelance practitioners producing either garments or swatches gain contracts through commercial agencies. Commercial agencies usually supply a consultancy service for clients that covers trend, yarn development, colour, mood and product boards, and develop trend-aware knitted swatches for a specific market, such as high street to high end for the women's, men's, kids', accessories and homeware markets. Clients using these services include yarn spinners, retailers, manufacturers and trade organizers. When approaching an agent for possible commissions, find out as much as possible about the agency and their clients. Make sure you prepare a portfolio of work that demonstrates your versatility as a designer and gives a comprehensive overview of your abilities, including the machines you are capable of working with, your knowledge of techniques and sensibility of colour, texture and detail (see Further Reading and Useful Resources, p.204). |
| KNITWEAR BUYER | Knitwear buyers often come from strong retail and business backgrounds. To be successful a buyer must be commercially minded, have a full understanding of the market and the competition, and an excellent knowledge of forthcoming seasonal trends. A buyer may work for a high-street retailer, specializing in the knitwear category for menswear, women's casualwear or children's knitwear for a particular brand. A buyer must have a good understanding of that brand in order to identify what will sell and what fits into their range, so as to build and develop the brand's image. They must work well within a buying team and work closely with management and merchandisers who assist in developing a marketable range that will maximize sales and profits. |

Visitors to Pitti Filati, one of the main international events for the yarn industry, promoting trends, yarns, research and developments within the industry.

# MAJOR EXHIBITIONS AND TRADE FAIRS

If you are seeking employment in the fashion and textile industry there are many major exhibitions and trade fairs that are worth attending, where you can find helpful networking opportunities. For new UK graduates Graduate Fashion Week and New Designers are excellent launch pads. Graduate Fashion Week acts as a showcase for emerging fashion design talent and is recognized as a catalyst for launching designers' careers and attracting major sponsors such as Topshop, River Island, L'Oréal Professional, Mulberry and many other prestigious names.

New Designers, held at the Business Design Centre in London, is an event that attracts over 3,500 graduates from all areas of design, who use this as a platform to exhibit their work. It helps launch many graduate careers and establish collaborations between universities, colleges and industry. It draws an audience of practitioners, industry specialists, companies, sponsors and the general public.

## INTERNATIONAL GRADUATE RECRUITMENT

Another option if you are a recent graduate is to submit a portfolio of work illustrating your range of skills to relevant databases such as Arts Thread, who present a 'weekly round-up of new portfolios, courses/programmes, student/graduate shows, design exhibitions and competitions', and act as a 'recruitment consultancy specializing in placing creative graduates worldwide' and offer an online service for designers and industry providing global links and contacts.

For further information relating to relevant associations and international designer networks see Resources (p.200).

## NATIONAL AND INTERNATIONAL KNITTING TRADE EVENTS

There are also many specialist national and international knitting trade events, from Première Vision (PV) and Première Vision Pluriel and Expofil in Paris, the Italian yarn show Pitti Immagine Filati in Florence, Yarn Expo in China to the New York SPINEXPO event and Texworld USA. The major trade events are open to international fibre and yarn manufacturers, while other trade events, such as the international exhibition ShanghaiTex in China, act as a global platform for manufacturers of both textile machinery and textile products, promoting the very latest in industrial machinery – circular, flat and warp knitting machines, and auxiliary and finishing machinery and accessories. All the main trade shows attract thousands of international visitors, including importers, exporters, retailers, wholesalers, manufacturers, agents, department stores and other related professionals.

Additional highlights of many trade events include fashion shows, trend presentations providing the latest news in fibres,

Top: International trade events, such as Pitti Immagine Filati, attract designers, manufacturers, retailers and buyers, providing the latest updates on what's happening in the industry.

Middle: Knitted fabrics exhibited alongside the latest news and developments in fibres, yarns, samples and fabrics at Pitti Immagine Filati.

Bottom: Fabric and yarn sourcing at Pitti Immagine Filati – reviewing the latest developments in fibres, yarns, construction techniques, alongside seasonal trends giving an overview of the industry.

yarn developments, fabric concepts, key seasonal colours and trends in knitwear stitch, silhouette and detailing. Seminars, displays and business and press meetings also provide excellent networking opportunities.

By attending trade fairs and exhibitions, you will keep up to date on industrial developments and new ideas, receive an insight into the way trends are moving, gain valuable sourcing opportunities, and make new contacts ranging from yarn manufacturers to accessory suppliers. This type of information is invaluable. Many yarn suppliers are now dealing with smaller firms and companies. They are, therefore, prepared to deal with smaller orders requested by home knitters, small businesses and freelance designers. It is therefore worth approaching company representatives at exhibitions and trade fairs to request complementary shade cards illustrating their new yarns and promoting seasonal colours and stock ranges.

**Pitti Immagine Filati**, based in Florence, is one of the main knitting industry events in the international calendar. Exhibitors present the latest developments in yarns, sample collections, specialized products, trimmings, buttons and accessories, knitwear machinery, software systems, prototypes, trend consultancy and trend books. Areas within the exhibition include 'Fashion at Work', presenting the latest global trends from companies such as Stylesight, who provide a multilingual website offering an in-depth global analysis of forthcoming trends and present forecasting information for fashion and design.

**Première Vision/Indigo**, Paris, is an important event showcasing current and future fabric collections, presenting the latest fabrics and fabric developments, fashion news, seminars, shows and trend forecasts.

**Expofil**, Paris, is one of the leading exhibitions for the promotion of fibres and new innovations in fibre developments, yarns and knit. It offers a showcase for weaving, jacquards, circular knits, tubular seamless knits and hand knitting. The exhibition presents new yarn collections, trend and directional information and seminar presentations for the textile industry.

**International Exhibition of Textile Machinery (ITMA)** is an international textile and garment machinery exhibition, showcasing the latest in textile technology, processing, technical textiles and garment making. The exhibition is attended by manufacturers, mechanical engineers, distributors, importers, exporters, buyers, sellers, traders, retailers, factory and store owners, yarn producers, fashion and textile designers, and all professionals in the textile trade. The exhibition also includes a 'Research and Education Pavilion', a series of conference and seminar presentations discussing such topics as sustainable textiles, textile dyestuffs and advanced textiles.

**SPINEXPO** is an important fair, showing new technological advancements in machine knitting and knitwear designs, and the latest in fibres, yarns and knitted fabrics. The exhibition is supported by fashion shows, seminars and trend presentations showcasing the latest colour trends and trend stories.

2
RESEARCH
AND DESIGN

How do you begin to design a garment that is interesting and individual to the wearer? Where do you get your inspiration? What colours and yarns work well together? This chapter explains the stages of the knit design process, from developing the initial concept and ideas through the research stage to the exploration of a design theme. It discusses the importance of predicting seasonal trends, new colour stories and the development of new fibres, textiles and yarns to the designer in the creative design process. It looks at where designers get their initial ideas from, offering inspirational suggestions and showing how ideas can be developed from an original source to inspire the colour, pattern, texture and shape of a garment. To assist you in the design process this chapter includes a range of garment silhouettes that can be adapted and developed or used to inspire your own designs.

**Previous spread:** Garment design from 'Alien-inspired' Spring/Summer 2011 collection combining both hand knitting and crochet techniques by Lithuanian-born designer Laura Theiss.

**Right:** Fine-gauge, futuristic knitwear design by Alice Palmer with metallic silver stud detailing and accessorized with silver-spiked leggings – Autumn/Winter 2010/11.

# DESIGN CONSIDERATIONS

A collection is a group of garments or outfits that work well together in terms of colour, style and silhouette and can be coordinated to create a particular look for the season. Designers will often create their collections around a particular theme – this acts both as an initial starting point and as a source of inspiration while designing the collection.

One of the most enjoyable aspects of designing knitwear, whether for yourself or professionally, is the creativity used to develop and produce both the fabric and the garment design. Knitwear design is particularly rewarding because of its adaptability and versatility – with a little ingenuity you can design and produce exciting fabrics and garments.

**Below left:** Bold sweater textural dress with asymmetrical sleeve cuff detailing by Alice Palmer for her Autumn/Winter 2010/11 'Batman' collection.

**Below right:** Monochromatic knitted maxi dress with fully fashioned 'fin' shape contours also from the Autumn/ Winter 'Batman' collection 2010/11.

# THE DESIGN PROCESS

An important element of any knit design is the development of the fabric. This may be design-led, designing the fabric for a specific garment range, or it may be technique-based and more about developing the fabric before designing the garment or collection. When designing a fabric consider season, yarn type and properties, including colour, texture and stitch structure, and whether you will work by hand or machine and, if so, the type of machine. Many of the trend information services provide updates on the latest trends in fabric developments, including new techno yarns and fabrics, seasonal colour palettes and new and innovative developments in stitch patterns and structures. When designing a knitted fabric, garment or collection it is important to consider the following factors among others:

♦ What equipment are you working with – domestic or commercial knitting machines?

♦ What colour story/combinations are you going to use – a palette of complementary colours or contrasting colours, a warm colour palette or a strong, bold colour palette?

♦ What is the stitch structure – rib, tuck, cable, jacquard, intarsia or plaiting?

♦ What season are you designing for – Autumn/ Winter or Spring/Summer?

♦ Who are you designing for – individual client or commercial company?

♦ What is your target market/customer profile? If you are working as a designer in industry – for example, a large commercial company – you will need to have full knowledge of your specific target market to produce appropriate designs and products for specific purposes, or you may need to work in response to a project brief.

♦ What price range are you designing for – couture, middle market or high street?

♦ What age group you are designing for – babywear, childrenswear, teenwear, womenswear/menswear?

♦ What occasion are you designing for – daywear, eveningwear, casualwear or sportswear?

♦ What type of garment are you designing – sweater, sweater dress, gilet, coat, jacket or skirt?

♦ What style of garment are you designing – silhouette, style or design features?

♦ What types of yarn are you going to use – natural yarns, man-made yarns or combination yarns?

♦ What type of knitwear are you designing – hand knitted or machine knitted?

To answer all the above questions and to create a collection, a designer works through a design process. This involves working from a design brief provided by the client to the brand ethos or producing their own self-directed collection, promoting a forthcoming 'look'. Producing a new collection, whether as a designer in industry or as a student, involves an awareness of future trends, visiting fabric and yarn exhibitions and trade fairs to keep abreast of new developments within the industry, sourcing yarns and fabrics, producing moodboards, and sampling to produce a directional and appealing collection. There are many stages in the design process and most designers will work through a process similar to that illustrated in the chart opposite.

**Below:** Experimental ideas by Sundus Akhter, exploring surface treatments such as bleaching, stitch transfer, colour and pattern to create new and innovative designs.

# STAGE

# OTHER CONSIDERATIONS

**SELECTION OF THEME** →
Instinctive and intuitive stage
Trend forecasting
Development of previous season or
  merging and developing previous
  season's trends
Determine title of collection

*SEASON*
*Autumn / Winter*
*Spring / Summer*
*Mid-season*

**THEME ANALYSIS** →
Research (primary and secondary)
Moodboard
Sketchbook (document all ideas)
Colour boards
Fabric development boards
Establish customer profile (age, gender,
  market level)

*RESEARCH*
*Attend trade shows*
*Exhibition*
*Forecasting*

**THEME EXPLORATION**
Sketching
Collaging
Image selection

**GARMENT DEVELOPMENT** →
Sketch
Silhouette proportion, volume and detail
Two-dimensional to three-dimensional
Modelling on the stand
Explore shape
Design detail
Trims
Method of manufacture
Hand knitted
Machine knitted or combination
  of both
Type of machine
Finishing techniques

*YARN CHOICE*
*Structure*
*Technical characteristics*
*Season*
*Handle*
*Drape*
*Appropriateness for technique*
*Appropriateness for season*
*Weight*

**FINAL GARMENT RANGE** →
Number of and range of garments
  in collection
Cohesiveness of collection
Accessories
Styling of collection

*FABRIC DEVELOPMENT*
*Source yarns*
*Yarn choice*
*  fabric structure*
*Stitch patterning*
*Weight of fabric (fine-, lightweight-,*
*  heavy-gauge)*
*Sampling*
*Trims*

# CREATING, RESEARCHING AND DEVELOPING A THEME

Inspiration for design is all around us; sources of inspiration can be found in many aspects of our everyday lives, such as nature, culture and architecture. To create a collection or garment range many designers will also often be inspired by a topical theme – for example, a newly released period film, which may inspire a collection with Edwardian overtones or 1950s influences. To create a collection in this way it is important to research the theme thoroughly, gathering as much research as possible to provide a starting point for the design work.

There are many ways of collecting and collating inspirational imagery and source material for reference, from mounting inspirational and directional images and ideas on the studio wall and creating a stimulating environment, to working in sketchbooks and producing moodboards.

**Below:** Inspirational ideas for Mark Fast's Spring/Summer 2011 collection. Assembled inspirational imagery, fabrics and yarns collaged together on the design studio wall act as a starting point to stimulate new ideas, which can be edited as the design work evolves.

**Opposite:** Nature is an excellent source of inspiration for colour, texture, pattern and detail. Moodboard by Carol Brown.

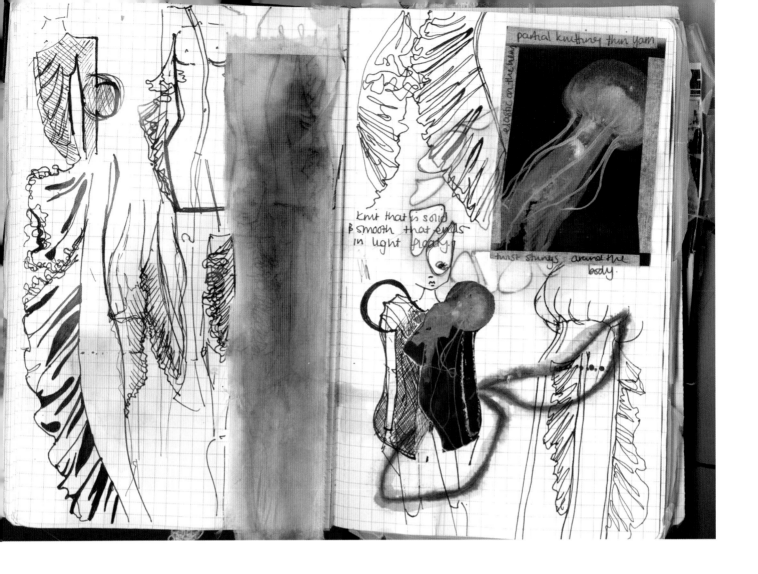

Some handwritten notes visible within the sketchbook pages:

partial knitting thin yarn

knit that is solid & smooth that ends in light floaty

burst strings around the body

**Above:** Example sketchbook pages by Amber Hards exploring the theme 'Fragile Forms' through drawing, colour and texture.

**Left:** Group of sketchbooks exploring ideas for colour, texture, patterning and yarn selection based on the theme 'Vintage Rose'.

# SKETCHBOOKS

Throughout the history of fashion design there have been many styles that have been heavily influenced by national and historical costume. From Paul Poiret's Middle Eastern-influenced designs to Vivienne Westwood's and Malcolm McLaren's 'Pirate' clothing. When using a theme as a basis for design work, collect source material, such as postcards and photographs, and sketch ideas based on books, magazines or artefacts. Try word association, stretching your imagination and exploring all aspects of the theme being used, to establish a starting point for researching areas of associated design.

Inspirational knitted and embroidered samples by Fumiko Kozuka.

Word association for the subject of folklore. The 'map' shows how quite disparate subjects can be linked by a common theme.

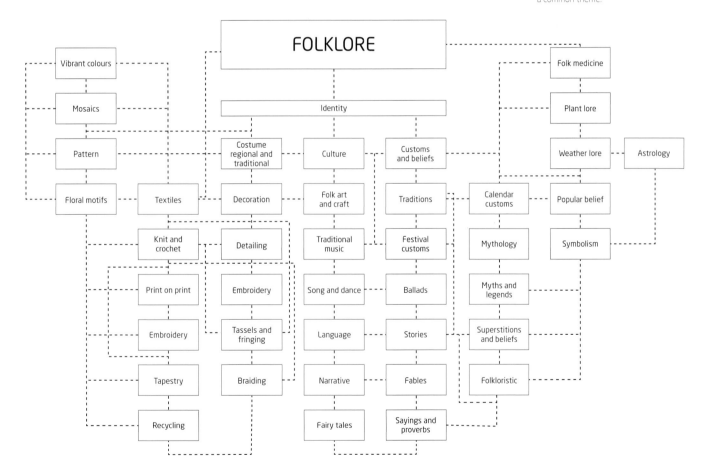

When beginning to design, a sketchbook acts as a valuable starting point for gathering, recording and analysing both primary and secondary research because it allows you to record your ideas instantly. **Primary research** involves collecting new and original information and ideas, which may include observational drawings, sketches, collages and photography; **secondary research** involves gathering research and references from a range of sources, such as the internet, databases, libraries, museums, galleries and archives. This can then be recorded in your sketchbook, forming a note of your ideas, which can then be collated, analysed and developed into concepts for fabric and/or garment design. A sketchbook can be used for your own personal reference or to explain an idea or concept to a client or lecturer.

When starting to record your thoughts in a sketchbook do not be afraid to sketch down any ideas that you find inspirational, thought-provoking or exciting. Do not worry about the accuracy of your drawings; as long as you yourself are able to understand the ideas then that is all that matters. Lack of confidence in your drawing skills should not inhibit you as a designer. Just sketch any ideas down, and through practice and experience your ability to record information and ideas visually will improve. Use colour, texture and yarn samples and indicate ideas for colourways, which will help you to make decisions and work out your designs. In the initial stages make preliminary sketches and gather images that inspire you. Try to develop challenging concepts through the exploration of various media to trigger new and innovative ideas. Make brief notes alongside your ideas where necessary. Compiling research in this way allows you to explore and experiment with your ideas as part of the design process, providing direction to your work.

There are many themes that can be used as initial sources of inspiration when designing knitwear. For example:

**Nature** – trees, plants, flowers, lichen, leaves, birds, insects, butterflies, wild animals, the seasons, the ocean, beaches, the undersea world, crustaceans, rocks, minerals, precious stones, mountains, forests, crops, rivers, lakes, climate, weather patterns and cloud formations.

**Architecture** – physical structures, buildings, interiors, exteriors, period architecture, the urban environment, bricks and stones, and types of architecture (for instance, Far Eastern architecture, North American architecture, ancient and contemporary architecture).

**Art Deco** – the 1925 Paris *Exposition Internationale des Arts Décoratifs et Industriels Modernes*, the opening of Tutankhamen's tomb in 1922 and the resulting vogue for all things Egyptian, Charles Rennie Mackintosh, Clarice Cliff, Paul Poiret, Sonia Delaunay, the Jazz Age, the flapper, the Ballets Russes – Sergei Diaghilev and Anna Pavlova – geometric patterning, stylized natural forms, Bakelite, lacquer and aluminium.

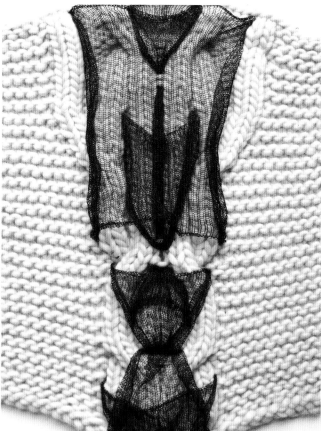

**Top:** Fine knit inspired by 'organic architecture – human bodies and insects' designed by Elena Muñoz Gomez-Trenor.

**Opposite page:** Design ideas by Elena Muñoz Gomez-Trenor, using the segmented body structure of an insect and the shape of the wings as an initial design idea, explored through drawing, fabric exploration and collage techniques.

**Top right:** The development of ideas from an initial source through to fabric sampling and development, playing with sculptural shapes and adding form and volume to the garment design, by Gemma Darby.

**Bottom right:** Design and analytical development ideas using tubular crin covered with knit to produce a dramatic neckline and bodice detailing, by Gemma Darby.

**Below:** Contemporary knitwear design by Gemma Darby – slimline fitted dress with ribbing and voluminous tubular neckline and bodice detailing.

**The seashore** – shells, crabs, starfish, jellyfish, sunsets, fish, seaweed, waves, sand (gold, white), sand dunes, salt marshes, barnacles, cushion stars, sea cucumbers, sea spiders, gem anemones, sea urchins, corals, tides, deckchairs, boats, fishing and ports.

**Fantasy** – fairies, elves, goblins, pixies, witches, wizards, dragons, fables, magic, the paranormal, the supernatural, magic, science fiction, folklore, fantasy, heroes, monsters, medievalism and literature (such as Tolkien's *The Hobbit* and *The Lord of the Rings*, Shakespeare's *A Midsummer Night's Dream* and J. K. Rowling's Harry Potter novels).

**The Sixties** – the Beatles, the Rolling Stones, Pink Floyd, The Who, Jimi Hendrix, Frank Zappa, Donovan, Janis Joplin, Bob Dylan, Joan Baez, Joni Mitchell, Mary Quant, Twiggy, Biba, Pierre Cardin, André Courrèges, Jean Muir, Zandra Rhodes, Emanuel Ungaro, Pop Art (David Hockney, Jasper Johns, Roy Lichtenstein, Claes Oldenburg, Robert Rauschenberg and Andy Warhol), flower power, hippies, music festivals, Woodstock, the anti-war movement, Eastern religions, psychedelia and feminism.

**Spanish** – flamenco dresses, frills and flounces, tiered dresses, spots, large flower prints and patterns, vivid colours, castanets, matadors, paradors, Spanish designers (Mariano Fortuny, Manolo Blahnik, Cristóbal Balenciaga and Paco Rabanne) and Spanish artists (Pablo Picasso, Joan Miró, Salvador Dalí and Antoni Gaudí).

The lists above illustrate the diversity of themes that can be chosen, researched and developed – the choice is endless.

Sketches and design developments of garment ideas using a combination of knit and woven fabrics inspired by the theme 'Seashore', by Caroline Prince.

**Right:** There are many stages in producing a garment or garment range, involving research and design through to the technical production processes.

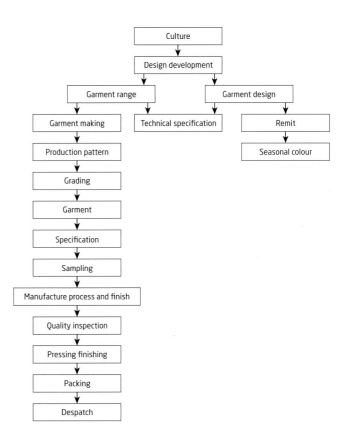

# MOODBOARDS

As part of the design process many artists and designers collate and stick down their research and reference material all together on one board, which is known as a mood, concept or research board. A moodboard communicates the theme through a collection of inspirational ideas and visually stimulating images, colour swatches, yarns and textures focused around the selected theme and presented in an interesting and informative way.

When creating a moodboard careful consideration is required in selecting, editing and using imagery so that your ideas are summarized and focused in a way that clearly communicates your theme and gives clarity to your vision. A moodboard can be employed to explain a concept in a presentation to a client(s), for in-house use or for individual personal use, as a summary of your inspiration prior to the design stage.

The size of the board can vary depending on its end use. If you are producing a moodboard to meet the requirements of a college/university project brief it may not state a particular size, so you may therefore match it to the size of your student portfolio – A2, A3 or A4. If you are working to a professional, commissioned brief and a moodboard is requested you will generally be directed to complete the work to a given size. For example, a moodboard commissioned by a spinning company to promote their latest yarn range may need to be A1 or A0 size for exhibition purposes.

When presenting your work, aim to create maximum impact by displaying your design ideas, colour stories and sample ranges effectively and professionally. Yarns can be presented on moodboards as yarn wraps or yarn tassels, and knitted samples can be presented with a sample header clearly labelled with the yarn type and spinner, stitch pattern, stitch count and any other details. Sample header cards with detachable hooks are available in a range of widths in packs of 50 plus from any leading supplier of manufacturing equipment to the fashion and retail industries. Alternatively, these can be made easily using quality card in widths of 30cm to 38cm for smaller samples or 46cm for displaying sample lengths.

Once you have collected the research material for your selected theme, you will be ready to analyse your notes and begin to sketch down some ideas, exploring your ideas visually, extracting colour and texture and building up pattern ideas. This will allow you to produce some samples based on the theme and, ultimately, a range of designs that can be translated into knitwear.

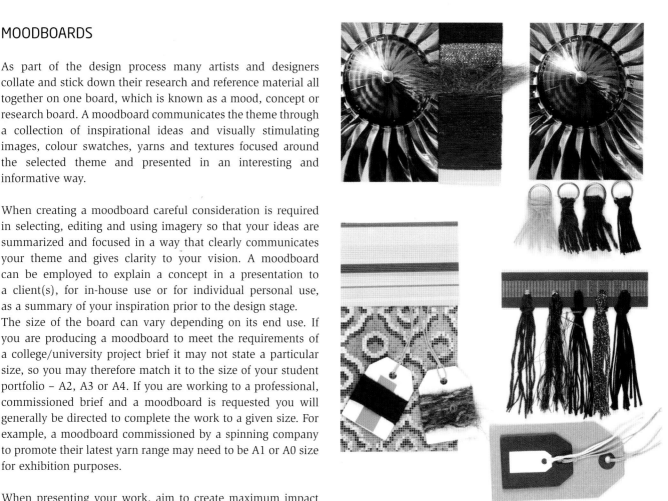

**Top right:** The professional presentation of yarns including yarn wraps and tassels, indicating colour palettes and yarn types can be included on mood, colour, range and final design boards, giving a professional finish to your work.

A natural colour palette inspired by environmental influences creating a colour palette of black, charcoal, steel grey, burnt umber through to cream.

# PLAY
## WITH
### CRAFT,
#### NOMADISM
#### AND
##### PRIMAL
###### URGES

Moodboard 'Play with Craft, Nomadism and Primal Urges' by Rory Jack Longdon, illustrating the cultural influences and inspiration of traditional costumes of nomadic tribes.

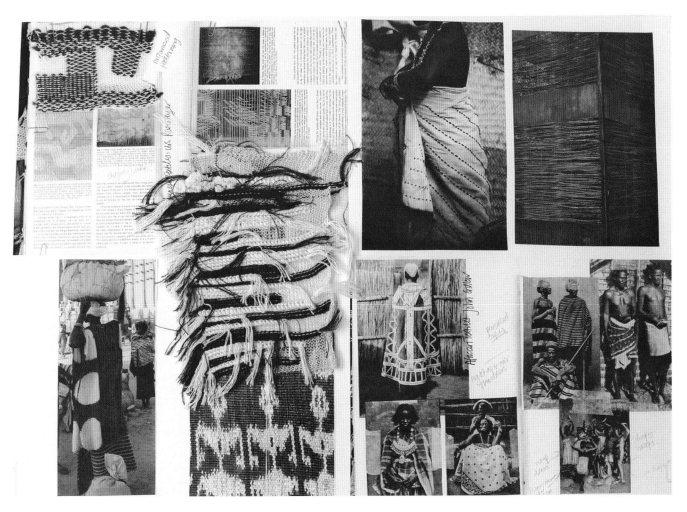

Research board by Rory Jack Longdon illustrating the cultural references relating to fabric, patterning and silhouette, selected as a source of inspiration for designing a collection.

The following examples of work illustrate the steps involved when using a single theme as a basis for a series of designs. They show the development through the research process – producing a moodboard, design sketches and knitted samples through to the point where final designs emerge, resulting in a knitwear garment or garment range.

Development of garments is also known as range building. When developing a range consider season, customer profile, how many garments are required in the range and how the garments work together to create a cohesive collection.

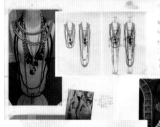

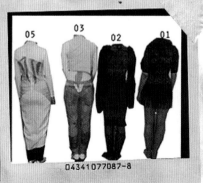

04341077087-8

04341077087-8

**Top:** Inspirational ideas by Beatrice Korlekie Newman, drawing on the theme of the Russian Tsars and 1,001 Arabian Nights to design a collection of garments using knitwear combined with hand techniques such as macramé and crocheting.

**Left:** The same theme as above worked in a range of luxurious yarns to create elegant and contemporary fashion pieces.

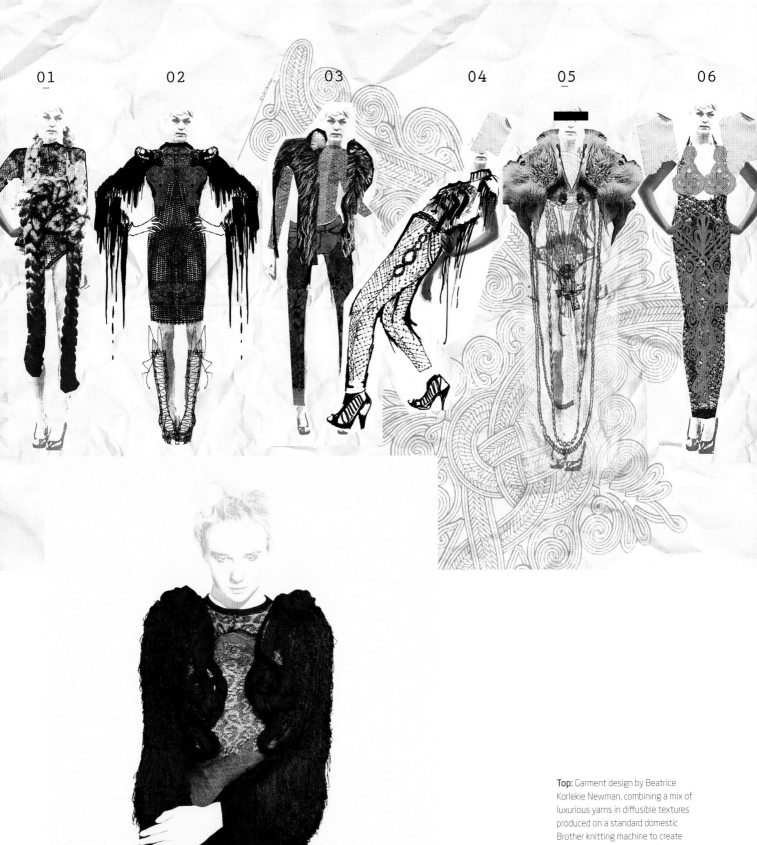

01 02 03 04 05 06

**Top:** Garment design by Beatrice Korlekie Newman, combining a mix of luxurious yarns in diffusible textures produced on a standard domestic Brother knitting machine to create elegant and contemporary bespoke fashion pieces.

**Left:** Illustration from the collection 'Tsars and 1,001 Arabian Nights', displaying the contrast in fabric development, texture and design by Beatrice Korlekie Newman.

# PREDICTING TRENDS – FASHION AND KNIT TREND FORECASTING

Fashion changes from season to season, bringing new silhouettes, styling and detailing. Many designers refer to trend predictions for colour and thematic guidance, while others rely on their instincts, working intuitively with colour, texture, stitch structure and silhouette, and often with references relating to their previous season's collection. In the process of designing you need to be aware of new trends in knitwear and fashion design. You should also study commercially designed knitwear shapes and styling, and what's happening within the industry, and keep an eye on new developments in technology and yarn production.

Seasonal trend directions offer new looks and ideas in themes, colours, styles and silhouettes. Trend forecasting is based on a careful analysis of the fashion and textile directions of the previous season, runway shows, street fashion, retail trends, demographics, consumer lifestyles and social and economic changes. Trend predictions provide a critical insight into the global market. Some companies work with sociologists and psychologists, who assist in the analysis of consumer trends and lifestyles.

Fashion forecasting is a very competitive business, researching and predicting international seasonal trends up to 18–24 months in advance of the marketplace. Trend information is used in the fashion, textiles, interiors, cosmetics and production industries, usually providing guidance on thematic stories, directional colour palettes, styling, detailing, fabrics, prints, yarns, trimming directions and graphic design ideas. Many forecasting services are available, giving seasonal styling predictions ahead of the season – some services provide twice-yearly forecasts (Autumn/Winter and Spring/Summer), while others provide monthly reviews of the changing and fast-developing fashion, textile and retail world.

Many prediction companies publish specialist trend books aimed at a selective area of the market: womenswear, menswear, childrenswear, the teen market, knitwear, bridal/eveningwear, contour/lingerie, sportswear, knitted, woven and printed fabrics, footwear and accessories. Trend information is used by major high-street designers, manufacturers' retailers, stylists' buyers and advertising and marketing companies to understand the direction of fashion and help them to set targets by predicting the likely future course of sales, promotional plans, changes in the market and consumer buying. Alongside the publication of trend books, many forecasting companies offer regular online trend reports, news and updates, which are available on a subscription basis.

Specialist knitwear trend books report any changes within the industry, and promote the development of new themes and colour stories resulting from the introduction of new fibres, textiles, yarns, fabrics and trims by yarn and spinner

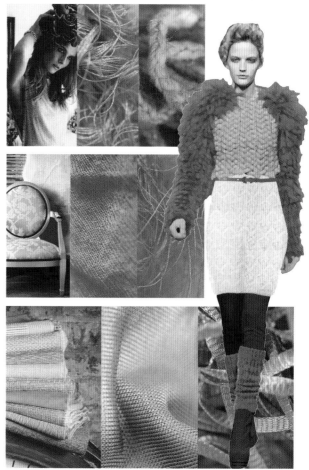

manufacturers. Usually a minimum of four seasonal themes are promoted. For Spring/Summer 2013 SPINEXPO, the international trade fair held in Shanghai, China, and New York, which promotes fibres, yarns, knitwear and knitted fabrics, promoted a series of trends under the umbrella title 'Universal Transformation'. The themes illustrated were: Cosmic Transformation, Aquatic Transformation, Cultural Transformation and Nomadic Transformation, offering four very different colour palettes and themes. These themes played on the notion of our immediate surroundings being exhausted as an inspiration reference, and thus encourage, 'looking further into new worlds, into space, underwater, the arts and hidden cultures' for inspiration instead.

Many trend books contain samples of yarns, fabrics and trims. The trends identify the season's key yarns, finishes and appearances, stitch structures and decorative treatments, with references to colour palettes (for example, PANTONE® colour, considered a colour authority), providing accurate cross referencing for consistency of colour matching globally.

There are many international forecasting companies, including WGSN (Worth Global Style Network), Carlin International, Nelly Rodi, Peclars, Sacha Pacha, Nigel French, Trendstop. com and Style.com. A more complete list of trend prediction companies and contact details appear at the back of this book. Many trend consultancy services offer statistical data and a wide range of market analyses, publications and reports, often in conjunction with online forecasting trend services and runway reports. Other services offered often include live presentations of trend reports at trade fairs and conferences, as well as the publication of regular newsletters providing mid-season updates and business news.

Industrial trade journals, publications and websites keep readers well informed of business issues. They provide regular updates on developments within the industry via the latest trend forecasts, coverage of the international catwalks, events calendars, the latest information on international trade shows and conferences, forums, sales data and features. Excellent journals include *Drapers* (UK), *International Textiles*, *Textile View*, *View on Colour* and *Women's Wear Daily*.

51-55 SPINEXPO Textiles Trends Autumn/Winter 2012/13, illustrating themes, colour directions, fibres, yarns, fabrics, trims and technical textiles. Each trend predicted provides an inspirational summary of the theme.

# DEVELOPING AND SKETCHING IDEAS

When developing your design ideas, consider the initial thematic inspiration, whether taken from a forthcoming trend or an intuitive idea. Analyse your research, moodboard, yarn selection and fabric concepts, and carefully consider the elements of your ideas and collected resource material. There may be a definite shape that you want to develop further. For example, the shape of foliage may translate into a design for the bodice of a dress, entwining the body in a lace-knitted fabric, or the wings of an insect may turn into an accordion-pleated sleeve. Look at shape, silhouette, scale, proportion, coordinating and contrasting colour palettes, and explore the detail. Take one or two main features from your visual resource material and develop them further into the design of a fabric or a garment shape. Be creative in your thoughts and let your ideas flow.

When starting to design knitwear, begin by thinking of basic shapes. The simplest sweater consists of four rectangles, comprised of two rectangles for the body, front and back, and two rectangles for the sleeves. These four rectangles make up the basic dropped-sleeve, slash-neck sweater shape. The body pieces have no shaping where the sleeves are attached, producing an easy-to-knit shape, perfect for experimenting with various colour combinations and/or stitch patterning. This basic sweater can then be adapted and changed depending on your knitwear skills, giving you a good understanding of how to translate your ideas.

Many of the designs in this book use simple silhouettes with intricate patterning and detail, incorporating exciting colour combinations and stitch patterns. When first designing it is recommended that you keep the garment shape simple and concentrate on pattern and colour usage. The best results are usually achieved by using simple shapes, as complicated silhouettes can often distort the patterning and appear overworked.

**Above and below:** Moodboard, design developments and technical drawings illustrating the design thought process by Amy Komocki.

There are many ways of sketching out your design ideas:

◆ Using a template of a garment shape and drawing around it, changing and adapting it and thinking freely about the silhouette as you develop your ideas

◆ Collaging your ideas onto figures from magazine adverts or photographs to illustrate your concepts

◆ Sketching out your design freehand, either as a garment shape or drawn on to a sketched figure

◆ Working three-dimensionally by draping fabric or moulding and manipulating paper on a mannequin or dress stand, exploring volume and shape

It is useful to record all the stages of the design process by photographing or photocopying your ideas and dating your work for future reference and further development.

The basic dropped-sleeve, slash-neck sweater is a popular shape today and reminiscent of the 1950s 'sloppy Joe' look. It is easy to change this basic design by altering the garment length, neckline, sleeve head, sleeve length, cuffs, ribs and pocket detailing. The diagram below can be used as a basic template to explore your design ideas as you work step by step through the design development process.

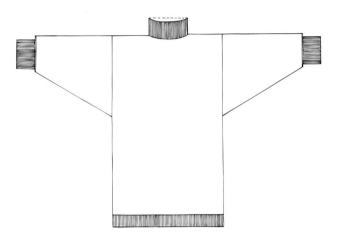

**Above:** Basic dropped-sleeve sweater comprising two rectangles for the front and back of the garment, and two rectangles for the sleeves, which narrow at the wrists.

**Below:** Design development exploring ideas and concepts by Rachael Hewson, who received an award for her collection at Textprint.

At the outset when designing, always experiment with design-development sketches. From your thematic ideas and early sketches, photographs and collages, consider concepts for **silhouette**. This is the process of sketching down ideas and gradually changing one or two elements of the design to explore a range of ideas developed from an initial starting point. Consider all elements of the design – the garment front, back, side view and detailing. By working through the design process, once you have sketched down several ideas from the initial design, you will see how the design has been altered. You will then be able to start refining and editing your work.

Using this simple process you will build up a series of design shapes and ideas that you will be able to use time and time again. All designers have their favourite **style lines**. You may find it useful to collect garment pictures taken from magazines that you can refer to for inspiration when designing, giving you greater understanding of the scope for developing ideas in shape and detailing.

**Above:** Fitted, body-conscious, highly embellished viscose knitted dress from Mark Fast Autumn/Winter 2010/11 collection, modelled at London Fashion Week on plus-size models.

**Below:** Contemporary designs in jersey and knit for a Spring/Summer capsule collection, inspired by surf culture, by Lauren Sanins.

**HELMUT LANG**

# STYLE DIRECTORY

The following style directory provides a selection of classic garment shapes and a range of sleeve, cuff and neckline variations. These are intended as a guide only, but they may help you in starting to develop your design ideas.

All-white dress that explores volume and structure using a range of synthetic yarns combined with cashmere and Lycra designed by Taiwanese fashion knitwear designer Shao Yen Chen, Autumn/Winter 2010/11 'Waver' collection.

# SILHOUETTE STYLES

# T-SHAPE SILHOUETTE

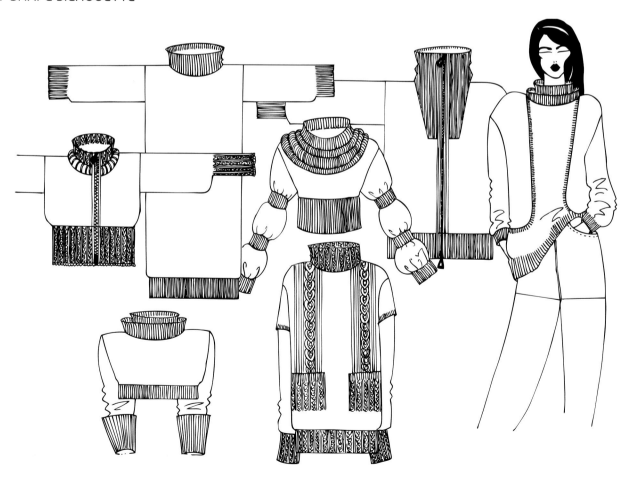

Chunky-knit, T-shape dress with exaggerated moss-stitch knitted bodice by Shao-Chen Yen.

# COCOON SILHOUETTE

# FLARED SILHOUETTE

CHAPTER 2: RESEARCH AND DESIGN

# KIMONO SILHOUETTE

# POCKETS

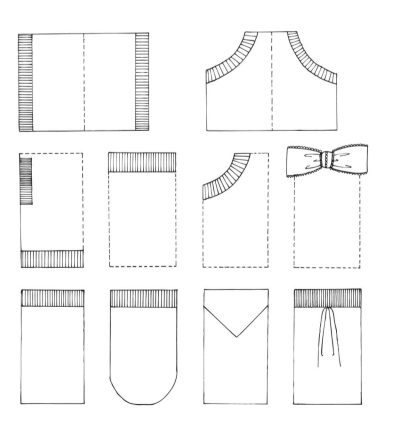

# FASTENINGS

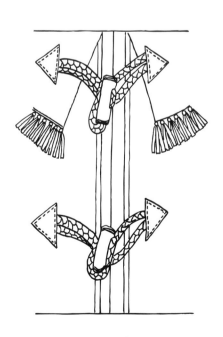

Women's knitted, figure-hugging dress by Maison Martin Margiela with exaggerated funnel neckline shaping.

Collar design detail showing the markings of fully fashioned shaping by Hannah Risdon.

# SHOULDER AND ARMHOLE SHAPING

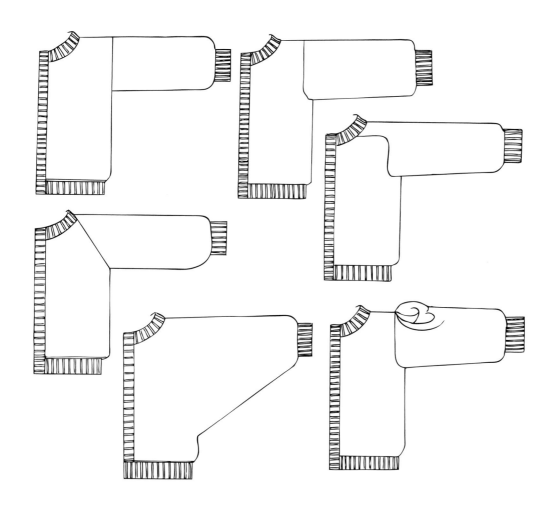

# CUFFS

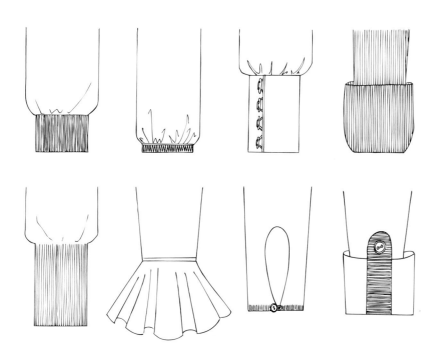

**Below:** Womenswear design featuring tube-knitted, looped shoulder detailing from the Autumn/Winter 2010/11 'Bugs and Butterflies' collection by Stine Ladefoged.

**Top right:** Structured, architectural knit from the Autumn/Winter 2009/10 'Control C' collection by Sandra Backlund.

**Bottom right:** Knitwear and wool felted by Monica YT Huang.

Fine draped knitted top with plaited neckline detail from the 'Imaginary' Spring/Summer collection 2011 by Stine Ladefoged.

Architectural, structured boxy knit with three-dimensional fabric with contrasting trim, created for Autumn/Winter by Burmese designer Steven Oo.

# DETAILING

Designs in knit can be traditional or exploratory, as illustrated in the ultra-creative work of Keiichi Muramatsu (below), who explains her concept as: 'Clothes are the canvas, material is the paint, and the designer creates with unbounded imagination'.

**Opposite:** Draped, textured knit skirt with deep-rib waistband by Steven Oo, Autumn/Winter 2010.

**Below:** It's all in the detail – innovative garment range focusing on colour, texture, structure and layering by Japanese designer Keiichi Muramatsu, founder of 'Everlasting Sprout' with Noriko Seki in 2005.

## CASE STUDY
# ALESSANDRA MARCHI

Tuscan-born fashion designer Alessandra Marchi works in both knit and woven, producing seasonal collections that are designed and manufactured in Italy. She studied a degree in Foreign Languages, and then she started working in the world of fashion, setting up her own fashion line 'Rose e Sassi'.

In 2008 she launched her Spring/Summer collection under her own name Alessandra Marchi, which has gone from strength to strength, receiving international press coverage in magazines such as *Elle* and *Vogue*. Alexandra sells her collections globally in boutiques in Tokyo, New York, Los Angeles, San Francisco, Moscow, Milan, London and Poland.

Her collections are very individual and her approach to design mixes traditional artisanal techniques with avant-garde concepts. Her garments explore silhouette, structure and movement with softly sculptured layered shapes enveloping the body. She combines the sensual, tactile qualities of fabrics and yarns such as stretchable silk, linen, pure wool, cashmere and technical fabrics for luxurious comfort and sophistication. Her designs, from jackets and sheath dresses to cardigans and jackets cocoon and wrap the body, and combine the soft structure

of knit with contrasts in fabrics. Alessandra is renowned for her intricate garment details with interest from all angles of the body and contrasting silhouettes with lots of asymmetrical pattern cutting and Italian tailoring.

**How would you describe your style?**
My style is exuberant in combining aggressiveness and refinement. I like working with contrasts, the contrast between forms and materials is a personal trait. I like the rough contrast of a masculine unbalanced jacket with sharp cuts and peaks, combined with a pure luminescence, stretchable silk, wools enriched with nylon thread in order to obtain a plasticized texture, and technical materials creating a 'harsh strike' with opposite materials that generate dynamic results.

**How important are fabrics to your work?**
I use interesting and contrasting textures, worked together in one garment and in one outfit. For example – a mohair net combined with a silk gauze, knit reliefs and wool enriched with nylon threads.

**Your designs show lots of attention to silhouette often through volume. How do you create volume in your garments?**
The silhouette is often defined by the volume and contrast in the shape of each garment, working together to create a strong look. The choice of fibre and fabric is paramount in creating volume, for example, a paper fibre that creates sculptural volume gaining movement, leather jackets whose unequal lines create the illusion of overlapped items with two or three collars or different sleeve openings, silk dresses featuring volume and movement emphasizing a determined, yet unpredictable femininity.

**How would you describe your silhouette?**
Many of my silhouettes play on angles and my designs are very versatile in their wearability, being multifunctional – for example, a zipper transforms a sleeve into a hood.

**Do you show your collections internationally?**
I show my work in the international arena, this season – Autumn/Winter – I am presenting both in Milan and Paris.

**Do you continue to develop your own research?**
Yes, the development of my work is very important to me. My personal research involves elaborating unusual forms and dynamics, and exploring new and technical solutions, treatments and applications of materials, giving greater depth to my work.

**Top:** Contrasts in fabric with a layered asymmetrical wrapped knit by Alessandra Marchi.

**Bottom:** Softly structured, layered hooded jacket combining knit, leather and woven fabrics with chunky zipper detailing for Autumn/Winter 2010/11 collection by Alessandra Marchi.

# 3
# WORKING WITH
# COLOUR AND
# TEXTURE

The knit designer is a creator of fabrics, and yarn choice is vital to the fabric development process. This chapter explains the importance of yarn selection, working with colour and texture, and identifying the various types of yarn available, from natural, synthetic and combination yarns to speciality yarns. Allied to yarn choice is the impact of colour and texture, so this chapter will also illustrate the practice of developing colour palettes and theme ideas from inspirational source material, and discuss the role of colour forecasting in fashion and design today. Finally, it will look at how to create texture and structure through surface manipulation and the application of traditional and non-traditional three-dimensional techniques.

**Previous page:** Issey Miyake ready-to-wear collection for Autumn/Winter 2010/11 comprising vivid, layered loops of knits in green, mauve, purple, navy, Dartmouth green, Persian red and apricot in pleated structures contrasting with black pants with drape and gather detail.

**This page:** Unique designs by Missoni, the Italian family-owned knitting company, in textured layers combining jerseys and ribs with heavily fringed knits in a stunning colour palette of bronze, copper and dark chestnut accessorized with gold chains.

# UNDERSTANDING YARNS

The variety of yarns available today is vast; they are available in an amazing range of fibres, colours and textures. Advances in yarn manufacture have led to the development of new and unusual yarns, which are readily available in retail outlets, online stores and direct from yarn manufacturers. When designing it is essential to have a good working knowledge of the characteristics and composition of yarns, as well as an understanding of the distinction between one type of yarn and another, as the fibre content, ply, structure and finish of a yarn can greatly affect its handle and the behaviour of the finished fabric.

## YARN FIBRES

Yarns are constructed of short fibre lengths (staple fibres) or continuous fibre lengths (filament fibres), which are spun, twisted or bonded together to form a continuous thread or length of yarn. These are made from natural or man-made fibres, or a combination of both.

Natural fibres from animal sources include wools such as angora, cashmere, mohair, alpaca, llama, merino and camel, as well as silk, quiviot and possum fur. Each fibre has its own characteristics. Mohair, for example, is a very durable fibre – it is lightweight but hardwearing, with excellent insulating properties and great elasticity. This fibre dyes well, retains colour and is often available in rich jewel shades. Cashmere, derived from the Kashmir goat, is a much finer fibre than mohair. It is beautifully soft and tends to drape well, which is why it is classified as a luxury fibre.

Natural fibres from vegetable sources include cotton, linen, ramie and other less common fibres – bamboo, corn, hemp, soy silk, banana, raffia and seaweed. Linen, which is derived from the flax plant, is popular for spring/summer as it is very cool to wear. It is a strong but luxurious fibre; however, due to its low elasticity it is often blended with other fibres, such as cotton, viscose and rayon, to create a yarn that is fashionable, cool and comfortable to wear with good moisture absorbency. Linen yarns produce crisp fabrics that are good for lace, cable and textured knitting because they show good stitch definition. Man-made or synthetic fibres include polyester, rayon, acrylic, nylon, bouclé and fun fur yarns, multicoloured space-dyed yarns that when knitted create self-striping knits, and metallic, synthetic blends and novelty yarns, such as Lurex. Man-made fibres are chemically processed and are often blended with other fibres to impart and improve the fibres' characteristics. Acrylics, which are one of the most common synthetic fibres, are often blended with other fibres such as polyester, wool and cotton. A typical blend is 60 per cent cotton and 40 per cent acrylic, or 60 per cent acrylic, 20 per cent wool and 20 per cent cotton. Acrylic is light in weight and is often sold in novelty textures, featuring slubs, knops or bouclé effects, or as chenilles in a wide range of solid, flecked and marble colours. Yarns are also developed by blending fibres or yarns. Blended yarns were originally produced to combine the advantages of

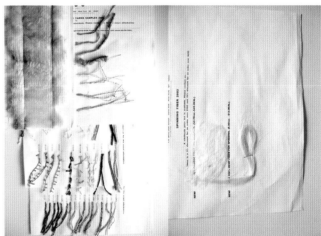

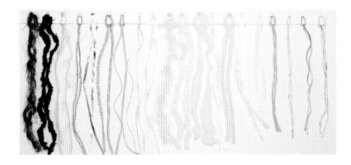

**Top and middle:** Experimentation with texture and form plays an important role in the designs of Nikki Gabriel, whose 'artisan' collections are handmade by studio production.

**Above:** A selection of yarns.

the selected component fibres. Blended fibres can also reduce the cost of the finished product and/or enhance its performance characteristics – for example, by increasing elasticity, improving shape retention, making the yarn easy-care, improving handle, increasing production efficiency, creating good dye ability, improving static resistance or addressing safety issues such as flame resistance.

In recent years there has been a return to the use of natural fibres for a couple of reasons:

◆ A greater interest in the sustainability agenda and the promotion of eco- and ethically-friendly lifestyle choices, which has resulted in a move away from the excessive use of chemicals. Many natural yarn blends have been introduced into the market, such as angora cashmere and silk. Seasilk yarn is another example. This is made by mixing seaweed fibre and silk fibre; its luxurious sheen is ideal for lace knitting.

◆ The increased cost of many non-renewable sources for the production of man-made/synthetic yarns and the resultant increased costs in production methods.

The last few years have also seen an increased interest in organic knitting yarns created from natural, ethically produced fibres. During the manufacturing process of these yarns enormous care is taken to reduce the impact on the environment, and great attention is paid to the care of any animals. The packaging of these yarns is also usually kept to a minimum; biodegradable bags, for example, are used to support the ethos of the yarn company.

**Above:** Close-up of garment design from the 2012 collection by Carol Brown, produced in Chinese pure bourette silk and 100 per cent Shantung silk yarn, offering contrast in texture and an exploration of collage techniques.

**Above left:** 'Prairie Dream' by Lexi Boeger, founder of Pluckyfluff. Innovative, quirky, hand-spun art yarn constructed in white Icelandic fleece using hand-dyed fibres, silk and embroidered fabrics, flowers, rubber cherries, and a doll.

**Above right:** Creative, textured, hand-spun yarns, also known as 'art yarns', constructed in cream fibres, netting and lace by Lexi Boeger.

## PLY OF THE YARN

The ply of the yarn refers to the number of single fibres spun together to form the thickness and weight of the yarn, which is often described in hand knitting as 2 ply, 3 ply, double knit (DK), Aran, chunky and super chunky. Yarns range from superfine gossamer weights of cobweb fineness, such as 1–3 ply yarns, which are a traditional favourite for lace knitting, to the other extreme of bulky 12 ply yarns. If you unravel a yarn by untwisting it carefully you will be able to count the plies. This does not, however, indicate the weight of the yarn, as a 4 ply yarn may be made up of four very fine plies. The yarn may also be spun very tightly, which will give a finer, smoother appearance.

## YARN FINISHES

There are many finishes that can be applied to yarns during the final production process to improve their texture, appearance, handle or feel, or to improve their performance and safety. Examples of finishes include dyeing, bleaching, mercerization (giving the yarn a lustrous and glossy finish), yarn twist setting, friction-resistant, flame-retardant and anti-static finishes, and heat-regulation properties.

## HOW TO CHOOSE YARNS

As illustrated above, careful consideration of the advantages and disadvantages of selecting a particular yarn for a project is very important. Fine yarns, for example, usually drape well and work effectively for many lightweight summer garments or garments that incorporate gathers and pleats within their design, while chunky wool is very good for warm winter cable designs.

There are many internet yarn stores that stock extensive ranges of yarns, including collections of natural and organic yarns. In recent years there has been a growth in the number of small businesses and enterprises producing and selling specialist yarns from individual hand-spun and hand-dyed yarns, alongside the larger mills that spin and sell their own brands, and companies that stock extensive ranges of all the most popular brands as well as speciality and novelty yarns.

All yarns should be clearly labelled, listing the fibre content, gauge or tension and shade dye lot number. When purchasing several skeins, cones or balls of the same colour always check that the dye lot number is the same on each item. At a glance the yarn may appear to be the same colour from one ball, cone or hank to the next, but the shade will vary slightly if the yarns were dyed at different times, and this will become apparent when the wool is knitted up.

Sampling and exploring yarns is an important part of the design process, giving greater understanding of the properties and the suitability of the yarn for the design, and also the best gauge to use. When working, it is useful to label each sample, identifying the details of the yarn type, tension and stitch structure.

**When selecting yarns consider:**

◆ The season – Autumn/Winter or Spring/Summer

◆ Who you are designing for

◆ The purpose of the garment or textile piece

◆ The price range

◆ The yarn properties and characteristics

◆ The stitch structure(s) being used

# WORKING WITH COLOUR

Colour plays an important role in the development of knitwear. Some designs work best in one colour, concentrating on shape, silhouette and detailing, while other designs focus on adding interest through mixing colours. Whatever experience you have as a knitter you can create fabrics by careful selection of colour. Even simple stitch structures can be made more interesting by combining colour in unusual ways. Everyone sees colour differently. Experimentation is important as this will give you a greater understanding of colour theory and the colours and shades that will work well together. Time spent understanding colour will give greater insight, stimulating new ideas when designing.

**Left:** Be inspired by colour, working and creating colour palettes by exploring and experimenting with single hues, contrasting colourways and proportion of colour using collages of stripes, pattern and yarn colour wraps.

**Above:** Garment design and accessories worked in soft colour combinations by British ethical knitwear designer Nicky Thomson.

# COLOUR AND MEANING

Tones vary in intensity, as illustrated by the four colour boards shown here and overleaf. In most societies colour is symbolic, although it often holds different meanings for different cultures. Colour is also often associated with different moods, emotions and ideas. For example:

Red: romance, passion, fire, warmth, danger, vitality.
Tones of red: scarlet, crimson, mulberry, pillar-box red, rose, fuchsia, magenta, wine, cerise, salmon pink, auburn, burnt sienna, cardinal, persimmon, ruby, rust, raspberry, vermillion, terracotta, Venetian red and coral.

Green: the environment, trees, plants, nature, spring, peace, emerald, jade, jealousy.
Tones of green: bottle green, emerald, deep aqua, acid, avocado, grass green, sea green, khaki, forest green, pine green, true green, viridian, racing green, olive, teal, and lime.

Blue: sea, sky, oceans, water, cold, icy, winter, sapphires, blueberries
Tones of blue: forget-me-not blue, lavender, turquoise, sapphire, ice blue, aqua, navy, royal blue, French navy, mauve, Chinese blue, teal, powder blue, Wedgwood blue, periwinkle, airforce blue, azure, cobalt blue, ultramarine, turquoise and cyan.

Yellow: sunshine, happiness, warmth, light, sun, summer, sand, beaches, wheat, corn, buttercups, primroses.
Tones of yellow: bitter lemon, mustard, tangerine, gold, amber, sienna, yellow ochre, amber, saffron, pumpkin, ivory, buff, manila, flax, maize, straw, old gold and buttercup yellow.

Neutrals: stone, cobwebs, metal, architecture, urban landscape, winter, cold.
Neutral tones: grey, dove grey, charcoal, pale teal, beige, blue-grey beige, warm beige, rose beige, ivory, buff, cream, soft white, oyster, sand, bamboo and taupe.

Brown: autumn, woodlands, earth, bark, camouflage, wood, hibernation, coffee beans, chocolate.
Tones of brown: spice, chocolate, cinnamon, nutmeg, ginger, peat, mahogany, coffee, rust, camel, buff, cocoa, beige, auburn, chestnut, hazelnut, bronze, buff, burnt sienna, burnt umber, raw umber, copper, fawn, taupe, sepia and tan.

Designers are constantly looking for new and individual colour palettes, which stimulate fresh ideas. Each of the following colour boards link colour with image and can act as a starting point for sampling.

Top: Shades of green from earth tones to lime green combine to create a colour palette inspired by images of nature.

Right: Harmony and contrasts can be created within a colour grouping, as illustrated, from the palest powder blue to cyan, Prussian blue, navy and turquoise.

The range of shades and colours of yarns available on the market today is extensive, from the subtle neutral shades of the true natural fleece to stunning, brightly coloured space-dyed yarns. Recent years have also seen a growth in the interest in the cultivation of dyestuffs from plant sources and the revival of historical dye recipes using madder root, safflower, goldenrod, onion skin, osage and indigo. When relying on nature for your colour, be aware that dye lots tend to vary considerably from one batch to another, although this can have the advantage of adding to the overall interest of the yarn or the garment produced.

One method of sourcing a colour palette is to choose an image as a starting point, and then experiment with yarns similar to the colours illustrated in the same proportions and colour groupings. Be brave with colour and you will be surprised at the effects that one colour can have against another, depending on the proportions and the density of tones. Each of the moodboards shown above/below links image with colour – associating colours, tones and textures with images to demonstrate the harmonies and contrasts within each colour grouping. Some designers work with colours intuitively, while others link colour to seasonal colour trends.

**Top:** Unique and individual colour palettes can be explored working with varying hues of the same colour such as sunflower yellow combined with mustard, old gold, primrose yellow, lemon and saffron.

**Right:** This board illustrates the wide contrasts in hue from the softest baby pinks through to coral and the rich saturated shades of pillar-box red, crimson, ruby red and maroon.

# COLOUR FORECASTING

Colour forecasting is big business and is important to many facets of industry, including fashion, knit, interiors, product design, the motor industry and marketing. There are many forecasting companies and associations who provide colour directions. The Color Marketing Group (CMG) is an international association that forecasts colour advice aimed at manufactured products and services; WGSN (Worth Global Style Network) offer a global online resource, including general fashion updates and colour direction, for design and product development, buying and sourcing; Carlin International offer a similar 'creative trend forecasting' service. Further details of international colour forecasting companies can be found at the back of the book.

Trend companies, as we saw in Chapter 2 (see p.54) provide the latest information and advice on colour stories for trend predictions, reflecting themes for forthcoming seasons. These are the result of months of research into new developments, trendspotting and understanding the movements and developments within the fashion and design industries. Colour forecasting companies provide colour information in the form of trend publications to inspire designers, brands and customers for forthcoming seasons. The trends promoted are divided up into colour stories, usually based on specific themes and moods. Fibre and yarn spinners and manufacturers may use this information as a colour resource to develop their product ranges and to generate yarn shade cards. These cards then work alongside the trend information to promote a colour and trend story, guiding the designer in the direction that fashion is moving.

When you start to design, experiment with colour proportions and pairings to create new and different colour groupings. There are no right or wrong colour combinations, and no set rules – often the most unexpected pairings will complement each other when put together in interesting proportions. A useful exercise in learning and understanding how colours work together is to wrap small quantities of selected yarn around a card and then play around with varying proportions.

Soft pastel, textured knits from Missoni's ready-to-wear collection, Autumn/Winter 2011 – Milan Fashion Week.

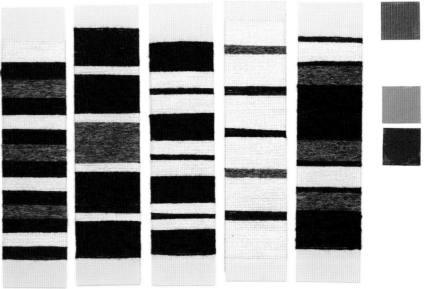

To explore colour proportions, wrap small quantities of selected yarns onto a piece of card to show the effect of emphasis when working one colour with another.

## STRIPES OF COLOUR

One of the easiest methods of introducing more than one colour into a design is the use of stripes in varying widths of colour. Stripes can be created using a very subtle blend of colours, hardly distinguishable from one stripe to the next, or for impact they can be completely the opposite – in contrasting bright colours that clash with one another.

If hand knitting or worked on a domestic knitting machine, a good tip when knitting stripes is to weave in the ends as you knit. This will save you many hours of work, laboriously sewing the ends in by hand or weaving them in on the machine. The yarn ends will then be securely woven into the knitting and only visible on the wrong side.

The Italian knitwear label Missoni is renowned for producing stunning knitwear featuring their signature stripes and intricate geometric patterning. Designs by Missoni illustrate the creativity that can be achieved by playing with colour. Designer Sonia Rykiel is also legendary for her exciting knits in kaleidoscopic colours and playful striped patterning.

**Above:** Collaged artwork by Hannah Buswell for planning out a knitwear collection illustrating block colour patterning.

**Left:** Bold, graphic and contemporary oversized knitwear, contrasting stripes with intarsia patterning by Hannah Buswell.

**Above:** Multicoloured knitwear in a profusion of bright colours by Sonia Rykiel, known as the 'Queen of Knitwear' – Autumn/Winter 2010/11.

'Electronic Sheep' by the Irish/ London knitwear label of Brenda Aherne and Helen Delany, who specialize in accessories, particularly hats and scarves with strong graphic use of colour.

Design development illustrating the initial concept for a menswear collection titled 'Shadow of a Doubt' inspired by the 'crossovers of train tracks and Hitchcock films' by fashion knitwear designer Genevieve Sweeney.

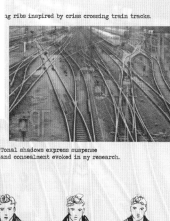

ng ribs inspired by criss crossing train tracks.

dramatic development in the collection.

Tonal shadows express suspense and concealment evoked in my research.

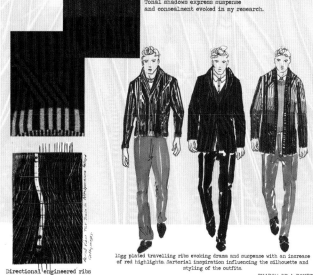

Directional engineered ribs

10gg plated travelling ribs evoking drama and suspense with an increase of red highlights. Sartorial inspiration influencing the silhouette and styling of the outfits.

SHADOW OF A DOUBT

FINAL COLLECTION

SHADOW OF A DOUBT

A model walks the runway during the Kenzo Menswear Autumn/Winter 2013 show as part of Paris Fashion Week, 2012.

**Below:** Bold, geometric, graphic stripes of varying widths in black, grey and beige colour palette with red highlights by Annalisa Dunn and Dorothee Hageman of Cooperative Designs, Autumn/Winter 2010/11

# FAIR ISLE/JACQUARD DESIGN

Fair Isle and jacquard are methods of knitting using two or more colours in one row of knitting to produce all-over repeats in a garment design. The traditional hand-knitted Fair Isle technique originated on Fair Isle, one of the Shetland Islands. This term is used very loosely, however, and is often referred to in both hand and single-bed knitting. Hand-knitted Fair Isle designs can be knitted in the round using a circular needle or alternatively using two or more needles, knitting the stitches and carrying each colour knitted along the row to form a repeat pattern, which can be relatively time consuming. Machine-knitted Fair Isle is quicker to produce, as the pattern is preselected using a punch card or by programming the design into the machine. Jacquard knitting is produced on a double-bed knitting machine, which gives a similar effect in appearance to Fair Isle knitting.

**Below left:** Relaxed, layered men's knitwear collection by Missoni with play of pattern on pattern and zigzags intersecting with checks, plaids and stripes.

**Below right:** Oversized men's knitwear by Kevin Kramp, which explores shape, colour and texture, worked in luxury yarns such as mohair, cashmere, wool, cotton, silks and nylons, in a wide range of colours and jacquard patterns.

## Experimenting with Fair Isle/jacquard

For the basic method of machine-knitted jacquard or Fair Isle, follow your machine manual, take a pre-punched card and experiment with different techniques. Play around with the punch card, sampling with different colour combinations, various weights and types of yarn, and trying smooth yarns alongside textured ones. Try experimenting using a Fair Isle design either as an all-over pattern or as a hem, a border design or on a single garment piece; enlarging or reducing the scale of the pattern also gives many design possibilities. Remember to note the needle selection mechanism while working. This experimental period will help you to understand and appreciate the full versatility of Fair Isle knitting.

Be aware that machine-knitted Fair Isle produces floats (the strands of yarn at the back of the knitting); this is not the case with the hand-knitted version, where the yarns are neatly woven in at the back of the knitting as you work. In smaller-scale designs machine Fair Isle floats will only travel across two to five needles and will not create problems. In larger-scale designs, however, the floats will travel across several needles and will be much longer and easier to catch, which can be problematic, particularly in children's knitwear. To avoid unsightly floats, alter your design by shortening the lengths of the floats or by latching them up while knitting. This technique of manually latching up the floats and hooking them onto the corresponding needles, though, can create puckering as the yarn is pulled tightly across the knitting. One alternative is to line the garment, neatening the inside and adding warmth and luxury to your design. Linings, however, are only appropriate for certain types of garment, such as coats, jackets, skirts and winter-weight items.

Jacquard knitting produces a more stable fabric as it leaves no floats. These are knitted into the back of the fabric formed on the second bed of the knitting machine.

**Top:** Chart for Fair Isle designs, which can be translated into hand or machine knitting.

**Right:** A range of samples produced in contrasting black and cream cotton yarns, demonstrating the use of the simple square and rectangle with play on geometric patterning, highlighting the simplicity and contrast in colour, and emphasis on the negative and positive.

**Opposite top:** Create your own Fair Isle design by graphing out a series of stripes consisting of small designs using squares, triangles, zigzag lines and small motifs.

**Opposite bottom:** Patterns for Fair Isle design can be drafted out on graph paper for translation for hand or machine knitting, and can be transferred to a punchcard or programmed into the machine.

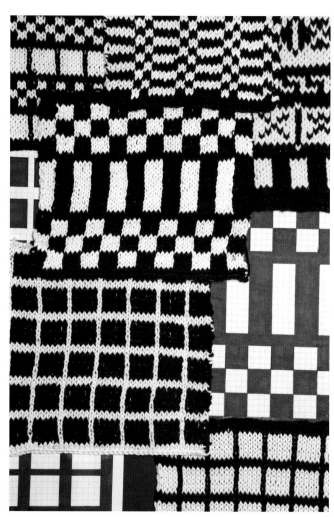

## Designing Fair Isle/jacquard patterns

Many knitters start designing by graphing out a series of stripes, consisting of small designs using squares, triangles, zigzag lines, crosses and small motifs. Any pattern formation that is repetitive is usually made up of simple shapes that can be used to create many designs, either using the shapes singly or combining geometric shapes together.

Once you have gained confidence you can then start creating more complex repeat patterns. Often the most successful designs, however, are produced by simple three- to seven-row patterns, with the emphasis on interesting colour work. Ideas for designs can be found in embroidery, textile and knitting books. These designs can be adapted to fit a punch card for machine knitting. The design created must be divisible by the number of your machine stitch repeat, which varies from machine to machine. On a punch card with a 24-stitch repeat, for example, the motif or design can be 2, 3, 4, 6, 8 or 12 stitches repeating across the fabric to create pattern formations. Alternatively your designs can be transferred onto graph paper for knitting by hand.

## Colour in Fair Isle/jacquard

To achieve the best results in Fair Isle or jacquard design, experiment with different levels of contrasting colour. To add depth to a design, for example, consider introducing a gradual change of colour from red to cerise through to magenta pink. You can create impact by working in clearly contrasting colours.

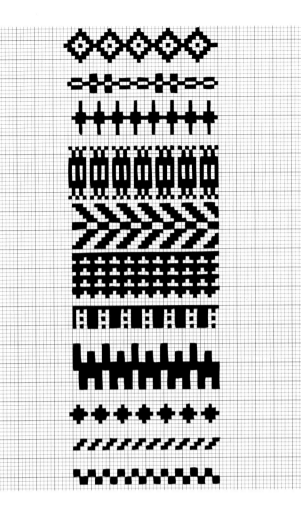

When designing your own punch card, important points to remember are:

◆ If the background colour remains solid, any hole that you punch knits as the contrasting colour. Simple geometric patterns as illustrated right lend themselves successfully to punch card designs, producing simple overall repeats. For the best results keep floats to a maximum of five stitches in length, otherwise they must be latched up or darned in.

◆ When marking a punch card for machine knitting, it is easiest to mark out the design prior to punching, to avoid punching the incorrect holes and making mistakes, which is easy to do. A chinagraph pencil, which has a soft lead, is useful for marking out the design on the card. If any mistakes are made, these can easily be rectified by taping over the punched-out hole. Always remove any excess tape, as this may produce errors in your knitting.

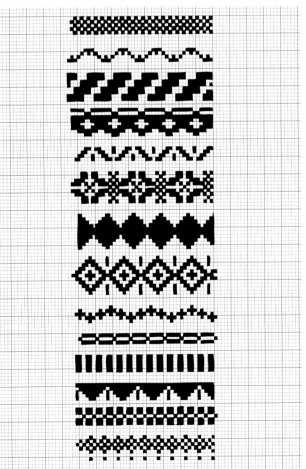

patterning in combinations of luxury and new technical yarns. These include cashmere, kid mohair, extra-fine merino wool, silk, metallic and retro reflective yarns and techno plastics.

Brooke shows at both London and Paris Fashion Weeks and regularly receives press coverage, having been featured in the *Financial Times* and *Fashion* magazine, as well as on websites such as Vogue.co.uk, Browns, WGSN, UrbanKnit, and many international site-specific blogs.

**You initially completed a degree in Applied Science and worked as a radiographer prior to studying Fashion Design and Pattern Cutting. What influenced the change in career direction?**
Radiography is fascinating but lacks autonomy. I loved fashion from when I was a kid but never thought of fashion as a career, until I moved to Sydney and met some Fashion Design students, and went to their graduation show when I was in the final year of my science degree. I knew I wanted to do what they were doing. When I moved to London I found my way into the London College of Fashion and Central Saint Martins. Now I combine my love of science and technology with fashion.

**Who or what have been your biggest inspirations artistically?**
Collaborating with Riccardo Buscarini (choreographer) and Elspeth Brooke (composer) at the Hospital Club, and developing ideas about fashion performance and cross-arts collaborations. I am inspired by opportunities to work in unorthodox ways, whether it is knitting from X-rays or presenting collections through dance rather than traditional runway shows. Digital knitting technology has been a major influence; transforming medical images into knitted fabrics by exploiting digital programming techniques and combining technical and natural yarns. I tend to look to the future rather than the past for inspiration.

**What's the concept behind your label?**
Science-inspired design. My label explores the links between science, technology and fashion, resulting in luxury knitwear with intelligence and experimentation at its heart. Robotics is an area I've been exploring since my SS12 collection and continue to explore with my friend and collaborator, Riccardo Buscarini.

**What is the most difficult part of designing a collection?**
Knitting is complex by nature, and every season I move in a new direction, using new yarns, techniques, and experimenting and developing new fabrics. Managing the budget is probably the most difficult part.

## CASE STUDY
# BROOKE ROBERTS

London-based knitwear designer Brooke Roberts studied fashion design at the London College of Fashion, and then studied innovative pattern cutting at Central Saint Martins. In 2009 she established Brooke Roberts Ltd, a new and visionary knitwear label that explores and challenges the knit process, crossing the boundaries between science, art and knit. She works as the creative director of the company, and as a design and technical consultant to other luxury brands.

Brooke's work is recognized for its intelligent approach to design, and its strong, technical understanding of knitted structures. Her designs are heavily influenced by human anatomy, medical X-rays and CT (computed tomography) scans, creating 3D cross-sectional images. Brooke's collections reflect her previous training at Sydney University, where she gained a BA (Hons) in Applied Science and became a practising radiographer. Many of her designs have a 1950s retro feel combined with cutting-edge technology. Owing to the high-level pattern cutting skills she applies to her work, many of her silhouettes are strongly tailored, with interesting style lines and stunning detailing.

Brooke's fabric designs are created using the latest technology, and consist of bold, graphic jacquard

### How would you define your style?
Sports-tech-luxe. I love bright colours and texture, sophistication and simplicity. I aim to make highly complex fabrics into effortless, easy-to-wear garments.

### How important is it to have formal training?
Training is important. I don't believe it has to be formal. Whether it's at university, an apprenticeship, or growing up immersed in a family business, what's important is the quality of training, and talent, not formal structure.

### What is your vision for your business?
I am currently launching Brooke Roberts Bespoke for several science and technology clients. I also aim to expand into menswear and open new product lines as the womenswear and bespoke businesses grow. I see my brand as a global brand for the future.

### What is the key to your success?.
Hard work, brand uniqueness and great mentorship.

### What is your advice to someone who wants to establish their own fashion/knitwear label?
Work for another designer first and get as much experience as you can. Be prepared to work seven days a week. Get a great mentor.

**Top:** 'Calibration' collection, Autumn/Winter 2011/12 by Brooke Roberts, who is inspired by 'an investigation of X-ray calibration films' and programmes her knits from X-rays and CT scans to produce graphic jacquard patterns.

**Left:** Knitwear design from the 'Calibration' collection, Autumn/Winter 2011/12 exploring jacquard patterning, combining a range of luxury yarns including cashmere, wool, cotton, extra-fine wool bouclé, silk, techno-plastic, metallic and retro-reflective yarns.

 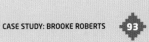

Work fom Bulgarian designer Marina Nikolaeva Popska's collection, Spring/Summer 2010.

Multicoloured jacquard design by Bulgarian designer Marina Nikolaeva Popska – Spring/Summer 2010, inspired by nature and light in a stunning mix of summer colours combining turquoise, orange, coral and the palest of pink yarns.

Menswear designs designed by South African designer Laduma Ngxokolo, combining local mohair and merino wool and inspired by the traditional style of Xhosa people and the rich patterning of zigzag, diamond and geometric motif designs of Xhosa beadwork.

**Left:** Industrially knitted and hand-cut fabric by Elana Adler, whose ideas are expressed through colour, texture, pattern and shape.

**Below:** Industrially knitted fabric by Elana Adler, a graduate of Rhode Island School of Design, US.

# INTARSIA DESIGN

Intarsia is another method of adding colour to your knitting that involves colour blocking, adding as many colours as your knitting design requires in any one row. This technique differs from Fair Isle knitting in that the varying colours are knitted in blocks and therefore the yarn is not carried across the back of the knitting as floats. This is an ideal technique for knitting large areas of several different colours, allowing you to create a design as simple or as complicated as you want: picture knitting, or knitting geometric or abstract patterns, lettering and large, bold design work. The emphasis of this technique is usually on colour and shape, with strong colour contrasts, as can be seen in the giant picture knits by Chinese designer Yang Du (see p.97). There are no limits to the number of colours that can be incorporated into a design.

Intarsia knitting can be worked by hand or machine. There are two methods of creating intarsia work using a machine:

◆ Use of intarsia carriage

◆ Holding position intarsia

The technique used will depend on your machine type. Some machines have a built-in holding position intarsia facility while other machines have a separate intarsia carriage, which can be purchased as an attachment. An intarsia carriage is an additional attachment for automatic or electronic knitting machines that replaces the usual knitting carriage and automatically positions the needles in the correct position for this technique. Always remember when working intarsia:

◆ To take yarns from the carriage side, allowing them to feed into the needles evenly

◆ When changing colours on a row, always twist the yarns, and take the second colour from behind the first yarn. This will prevent gaps from appearing between yarns.

When planning your intarsia pattern, sketch out your design and then transfer and plot it out on graph paper, one square representing one stitch. Remember that knitting stitches are not square; therefore, if you use squared graph paper your design will appear elongated when it is knitted up. Special knitter's graph paper is available from specialist suppliers. Intarsia knitting requires patience and concentration, as the more colours that are incorporated into your design, the more difficult and complicated it will be to knit, but stunning results can be achieved.

**Intarsia tension**

When knitting a garment with the design only on the front and back (with the sleeves in plain stocking stitch, for example), always remember that you will need to knit two separate tension squares to calculate the tension, as the tension may differ and need to be adjusted according to the stitch structure. For example, plain stocking stitch knitting may knit at a looser tension than Fair Isle.

# TEXTURE

All knitted stitches produce a textured surface, but the results depend on the type of yarn knitted, the tension, the stitch combination and the performance of the yarn. Once you have a working knowledge of different yarn properties, and an understanding of how one stitch works with another, you will gain more flexibility in your work. Textures in knitting can be created using any of the following:

◆ Particular yarns: bouclés, slubs, crêpes, chenilles, smooth silks, ribbons, tapes, faux fur, marled yarn, mercerized and speciality yarns

◆ Stitch formation: lace, tuck, weave, slip stitch or a combination of techniques worked together

◆ Three-dimensional knitting, incorporating ridges, bobbles, knitted flaps and cables

◆ Additional surface decoration worked into the knitting after completion, for example, embroidery, Swiss darning, appliqué and smocking

◆ Combining with other crafts, including hand knitting with machine knitting, crocheting or tatting.

Each technique is limitless in its potential as a creative aspect of design. One of the features of knitting is that there is always something new to be discovered and created. When exploring knitting and construction techniques it is useful to experiment with varying tensions, yarn types and colour combinations to appreciate the effects that can be achieved. Always make notes of your ideas as you work so that you can refer back to them, for example, recording knitting tensions and stitch patterns while sampling.

**Top:** Experimentation with texture and form plays an important role in the designs of Nikki Gabriel, whose 'artisan' collections are hand-made by studio production.

**Middle:** Sample detail of textured knit fabric by Carol Brown 2012, comprising black and grey softly brushed mohair, ribbon yarns, silver Lurex, and cotton and linen twist strands latched into the main base knitted fabric.

**Bottom:** Close-up of garment detailing, exploring weights of yarn, 2012 collection by Carol Brown.

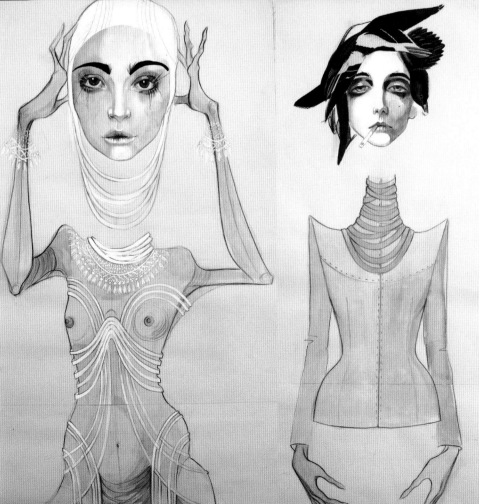

**Top left:** Highly textured design from the 'Tiki-Mani-Maori' collection by Danish designer Anne Sofie Madsen.

**Left and above:** Illustrations by Danish designer Anne Sofie Madsen showing her 'Tiki-Mani-Maori' collection, inspired by and translating the traditional Maori art of relief carving, Ta moko body marking and Maori spirals.

# SURFACE MANIPULATION

The knitted surface can be manipulated by applying a variety of techniques, from tucking, pin tucks, partial knitting and ruched effects to cable designs, each of which will add tactile qualities to your fabric. These techniques work well if a single colour yarn is used, which will emphasize the textural effect. Alternatively, a range of colours can be used when combining techniques such as tuck and Fair Isle design.

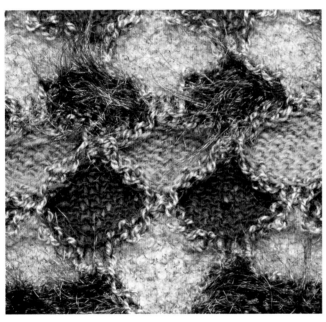

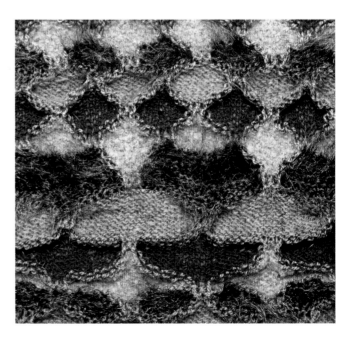

**Top:** Black and cream sample boards exploring surface manipulation through ruching, tucking and smocking, with highlights of red embroidery for contrast.

**Above:** Honeycomb effects can be produced through picking up the knitting at regular points, creating a versatile fabric with surface interest on both sides of the knit. This piece was

knitted in mohair, chenille and pure wool yarns by Carol Brown.

**Above right:** Surface manipulation using the technique of short-row tucks in mohair, chenille and pure wool yarns.

**Right:** Ruched fabric using the technique of short-row knitting in mohair, chenille, crêpe and pure wool yarn.

## Tuck stitch

Tuck stitch is easily recognized as it gives a sculptural, three-dimensional surface effect, and adds distortion to the fabric. Tuck stitch is produced by putting selected needles into holding position. This can be worked manually or by using the needle selection cams on your knitting machine. The yarn then collects on these needles, producing a tuck, giving shape and movement to the fabric. One or more rows are then knitted on all needles returning to normal working position, before returning to the tuck needle position.

The number of rows that can be knitted on hold will depend on the yarn, machine type, distribution of needles, and the tucking and pattern formation. If the needles do become overloaded with yarn, the stitches will drop off, so care must be taken when moving the machine carriage across each tuck row. To explore the technique of tucking, knit sample swatches to explore the full capacity of each tuck design. Produce samples using yarns of various thicknesses and on a variety of tensions to find those that give the best results. Many interesting and complex fabric structures can be produced by clever use of this technique combined with careful selection of yarn and colour coordination.

**Below:** Two-colour 'honeycomb' tuck stitch sample by Hannah Risdon, produced by holding selected stitches, while continuing to knit the remaining stitches as normal, creating a three-dimensional tuck, distorting the fabric.

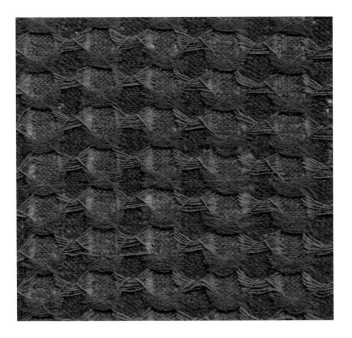

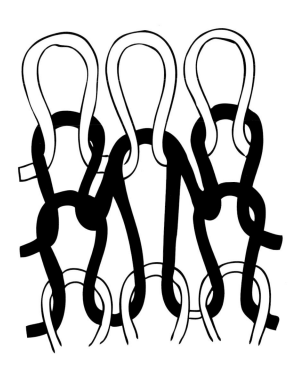

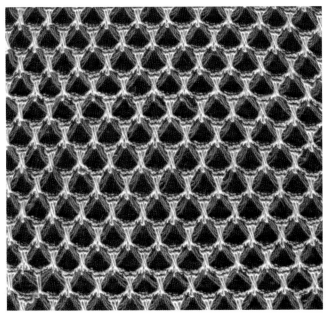

**Right:** Four-colour, 'circular' textured tuck pattern, created by Hannah Risdon.

## Ruched knitting

Another method of manipulating the surface is by ruching the fabric. Knit a length in the selected colourway and stitch structure, picking up selected stitches with a transfer tool. This can either be worked with regular spacing or the stitches can be picked up randomly. Ruched knitting produces a three-dimensional surface that combines particularly well with Fair Isle or jacquard designs.

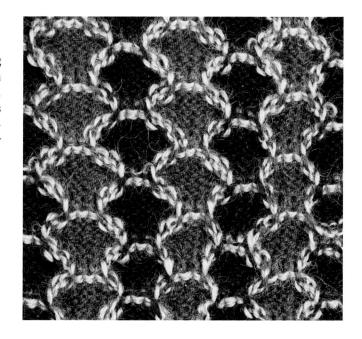

**Above:** Combined honeycomb and woven textured design produced in brightly dyed wool, Lurex and bouclé yarns on a domestic knitting machine, using a punchcard facility for automatic needle selection.

**Top:** Ruched knitted fabric produced on a domestic knitting machine by selecting stitches from previous rows and rehanging them on to the working needles, forming a ruched effect.

**Above right:** Simple striped knit, smocked at regular intervals and stitched into position and decorated with a cluster of couched knots.

**Right:** Highly textured sample by Carol Brown, incorporating irregular ruching, pintucks and lace detailing.

## Pin tucks, ridges and sculptured forms

Pin tucks can be used to add texture in a series of small ridges. They look particularly effective when worked in contrasting colours and textures, adding weights to the fabric, and also providing a guideline for picking up. Rows of pin tucks, when pinched together and darned into position with contrasting yarn, create a smocked ridge effect, as illustrated below.

You can also achieve sculptural effects by producing wide stripes of knitting in alternate colours on a loose tension, as shown in the piece on the opposite page centre right After pressing, manually ruche up the knitted fabric using French knots, working the embroidery in a contrasting colour to create a simple yet effective design.

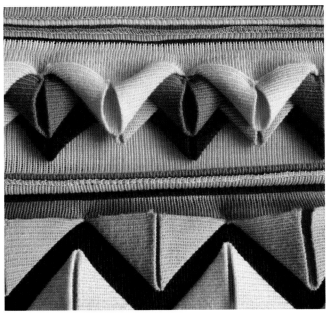

**Above:** Ridged knit design by Mark Fast.

**Top left:** Textured knit of ridges and bobbles by Jade Drew, inspired by rock formations, earth layers and Aboriginal art, using a variety of yarns for textural contrast.

**Bottom left:** Stunning, sculptural three-dimensional fabric by Jade Drew, inspired by natural structures of pine cones and seed pods.

**Above:** Layered textured knit by Rachael Hewson, using refined pattern, delicate tucks, ribs and manipulated details, creating gathers and blistered effects in tone on tone.

**Right:** Draped and layered textured knits in fine ivory, white and cream yarns by Rachael Hewson.

## Partial knitting or short-row knitting

Partial knitting is an excellent method of shaping a garment. It can also be used to add a panel or flair and fullness to a skirt or dress, or a dart to a jacket or sleeve, or it can be used to create interest by adding a panel in a different stitch pattern or colour into a flat piece of fabric, as well as three-dimensional bobbles, flaps, ruffles and decorative edgings.

This technique involves knitting selected needles and knitting only part of a row. It is worked either by selecting needles manually and putting them into non-working position or alternatively by using the cam controls and punch card, which then preselects the needles to be knitted. It is an effective technique for moulding and sculpting a fabric and can be used to add fullness to the middle of a row of knitting, to lengthen one side of the fabric, to form a dart, to mitre a corner, or to create curves or vertical gathers, ruffles and decorative trims.

Slitted fabrics can be created by putting needles on hold, knitting a row and casting off those needles on hold and then casting on and continuing knitting. In hand knitting, the same effects can be produced by knitting selected stitches, then turning the work and working backwards and forwards across selected stitches, giving greater fullness and shaping the knitting in a particular area of the garment, for example at the heel of a sock, across the chest, or to create an interesting sleeve design.

**Top:** Black and beige sample knitted in organic cotton and linen using short row tucks to create a three-dimensional surface structure.

**Left:** Short pin tucks and whole-row pin tucks positioned at regular and irregular intervals, produced on a domestic knitting machine, combine to create this heavily textured fabric by Carol Brown.

**Above:** Multicoloured dress with decorative slitted textured surface combined with partial knitting techniques and contrasting fabric underlay.

## Cables

Cable knitting, whether worked by hand or machine, adds real depth and surface texture to a fabric, and can be worked in isolated areas such as a design integrated into a ribbed cuff, or it can appear as an all-over cable garment design. Many traditional hand-knitting cable patterns can be taken and adapted for machine knitting. Cable designs are described by needle arrangements, for example 2 x 2, 3 x 3, 4 x 4. A 2 x 2 arrangement indicates the crossing over of two stitches with the two adjacent stitches; 3 x 3 indicates the crossing over of three stitches with the adjacent three stitches, and so on, worked manually using machine transfer tools. The design will vary greatly depending on the number of stitches crossed over and the number of rows knitted between stitch transfers.

**Right:** Cream knit cable sweater by Michael Kors, combining single and double twisted cables and diamond cable design.

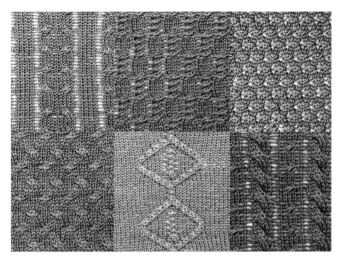

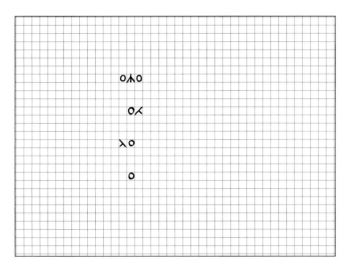

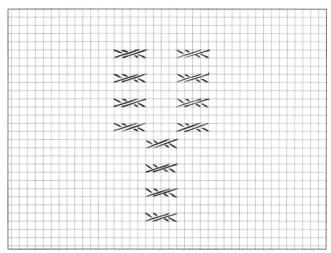

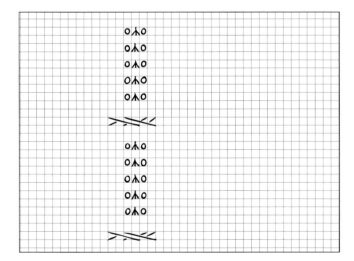

**Top left:** Manually worked cable samples showing a range of cable designs exploring various needle arrangements produced on a single-bed domestic knitting machine.

**From top left, left to right:**
(a) Double snake cable
(b) 2 x 2 twisted cable
(c) Travelling cable
(d) Shadow cable pattern

(e) Diamond framed cable design
(f) Combining cable patterns within one fabric

**Middle left:** Symbols for lace and cable transfer.

**Bottom left:** Chart for decorative eyelet cable design. Many interesting cable designs can be created by varying the number of stitches crossed and the number of rows worked between the crossings of stitches.

**Top right:** 2 x 2 twisted cable. The width of the cable can be changed by the number of rows knitted between each cable. When the cables are worked closely together, the width of the cable is reduced greatly, giving an interesting textured effect.

**Middle right:** Diagram for 2 x 2 cable twist design.

**Bottom right:** Double 2 x 2 cable with ladder row adding both ease and texture to the design.

Cable designs can be worked in one colour or combined with a multicoloured jacquard pattern, or alternatively with a tuck pattern or combined with decorative lace knitting. Traditional cable designs can be used to great effect by playing with scale, enlarging the cables and joining several cables together.

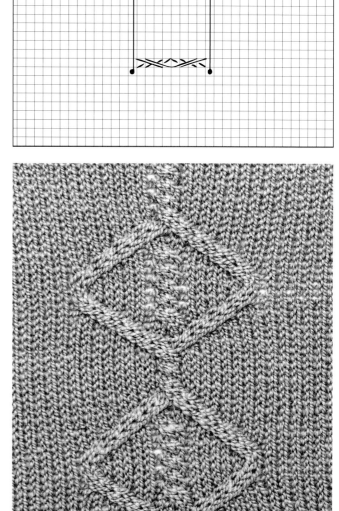

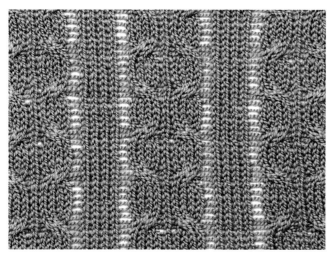

**Top left:** A basic 3 x 3 cable design with additional ladder row, creating a decorative feature and adding further texture to the overall design, which can be produced by hand or on a machine.

**Bottom left:** Double snakey cable design is created by working two parallel cables over seven rows with a needle in non-working position, giving a ladder effect and also greater definition to the cable design.

**Top right:** 2 x 2 double snake linked cable design with eyelet hole.

**Bottom right:** Diamond cable design produced by staggering a 2 x 2 cable pattern.

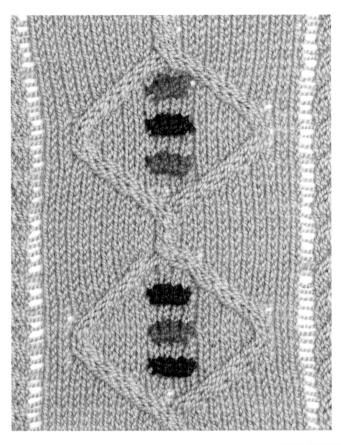

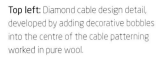

**Top left:** Diamond cable design detail, developed by adding decorative bobbles into the centre of the cable patterning worked in pure wool.

**Middle left:** Diagram for cable design.

**Bottom left:** Combining different cable designs together of varying structures crossing in opposite directions creates an interesting, staggered cable effect.

**Below right:** Eight-stitch, plaited cable design knitted in pure wool on a single-bed domestic knitting machine.

**Bottom right:** Diagram for cable design.

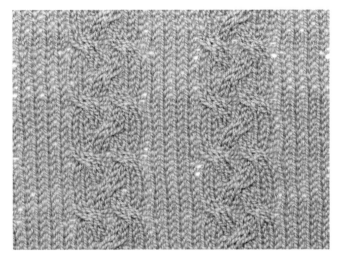

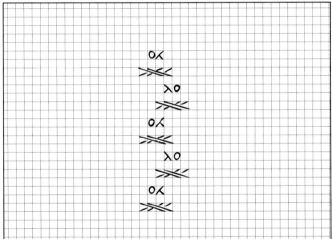

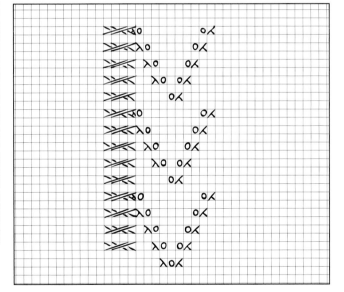

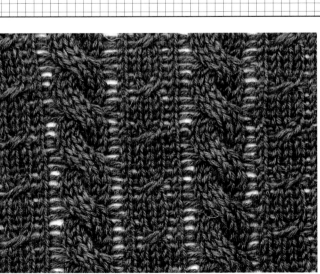

Start your sampling by exploring simple cable patterns – 2 x 2, 3 x 3, as illustrated on the previous pages, building your knowledge and confidence before exploring more complex cable designs. Designs combining the techniques of cable design and lace knitting work well together. Highly innovative fabrics can be produced through careful planning and experimentation with colour, texture and positioning of the cable design.

**Opposite:** Mock cable created by knitting lengths of tube knitting and plaiting together, and then stitched onto the finished garment, by Irina Shaposhnikova.

**Above:** Cable knit combined with web textures by Hannah Simpson.

**Right:** Cable knit combined with plaited knit by Hannah Simpson.

## Lace and laddering effects

Laddering or eyelet holes can be worked into a knitted structure to create extra interest. Eyelet holes are created by knitting two stitches together; ladders are produced by leaving one or more needles in a non-working position on the knitting machine. Ladder effects can be used to great effect by careful positioning or, if used as a base fabric, to thread ribbon, tape, leather thonging or cord through, adding to the textural quality of the fabric.

**Above:** Stunning design using ladder-knit technique for Spring/Summer 2010 by London-based Turkish designer Bora Aksu, who states 'My signature style is based upon finding the balance point between contrasts. It's romantic with a darker twist.'

**Below:** Spring/Summer 2013 design collection by Nicole Farhi, featuring ladder knit design by Carmen Leng.

NICOLE FAR

Stunning ladder and ribbon handcrafted knit created in metallic yarn for Spring/ Summer 2011 collection designed by Swedish designer Sandra Backlund.

CHAPTER 3: WORKING WITH COLOUR AND TEXTURE

## Lace knitting

Lace knitting has a long history and is derived from lacemaking. Lacemaking traditionally uses very fine threads and is very time consuming to produce due to the complexity of technique and pattern. Knitted lace grew in popularity during the twentieth century and has become a very popular substitute. Lace knitting is formed by the transfer of stitches from one needle to another by either hand tooling or by using a lace carriage, making a hole or series of holes in the knitting.

Lace knitting can add a delicate textural quality to a fabric and is ideal for eveningwear and summer wear. Ribbons can be woven through it, and it can also be decorated with bead embroidery. One or more of these techniques can also be combined together. Lace knitting can be worked on knitting needles by hand or knitted using a punch-card facility on a knitting machine. The manufacturer will usually provide a range of lace-knitting punch cards that can be tried and tested, adapted and developed.

There are many traditional lace patterns that can be modified and translated into machine-knitted or hand-knitted lace. Designs can be charted out on graph paper or, alternatively, written out.

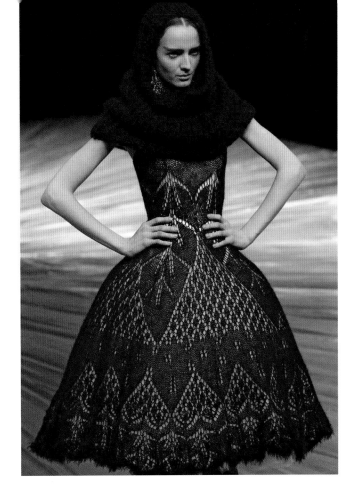

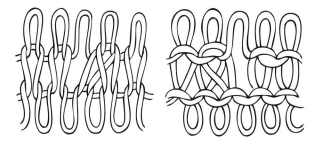

**Opposite:** Figure-hugging, crimson knit dress with intricate lace transfer and sleeve fringing by Canadian designer Mark Fast, who is renowned for combining Lycra yarns and natural fibres together – Spring/Summer 2009.

**Top:** Black fine lace-knitted dress with heart motifs and feather trim by Alexander McQueen.

**Bottom:** Black lace-knit sculpted dress designed by hand on a domestic knitting machine by Mark Fast, Spring/Summer 2009.

## CASE STUDY
# IBEN HØJ

Knitwear designer and consultant Iben Høj studied Fashion and Textiles with Business Studies at the University of Brighton. She gained further experience in the field of knitwear design, completing a work placement at the Marc Jacobs studio, and working as a designer for Knit-1 (formerly Dykes Enticknap) from 1997 to 1998. This work involved initiating and executing one-off styled knitwear swatches for womens- and menswear, which sold in Europe, the US and Japan, and at all the major trade shows. In 1997 she was selected and sponsored by the Texprint annual design exhibition at Indigo, Paris, and in 1998 she was appointed Senior Knitwear Designer at Bruuns Bazaar, Copenhagen, where she worked until 2002 on the main line and diffusion line BZR for both womens- and menswear collections. Simultaneously, freelance commissions creating swatches as mock-up garments sold worldwide to fashion houses such as Marni and Donna Karan. In 2002 Iben was awarded a business development grant by the Danish Arts Council, and established her own company, designing and producing knitwear. This involved developing new stitches and shapes, designing and managing the production, including quality control, presenting collections at international fairs and, finally, distributing worldwide. Her garments have sold in high-end speciality boutiques including Liberty, London, and Moda Key in Doha, Qatar. In 2004, Iben received sponsorship to represent Denmark

at the 'Creator's Village' during Tokyo Fashion Week, and since 2005 she has presented her designs at the trade shows during Paris, Berlin, Milan, New York and Copenhagen Fashion Weeks. Iben's work has received international coverage in books, magazines and journals and her designs have been purchased by celebrities including Kate Moss, Halle Berry, Helena Christensen and the Crown Princess Mary of Denmark.

In 2009, her solo exhibition 'Kraka's Dresses – Nearly Nude' at the Designmuseum, Denmark, resulted in her inclusion in their permanent dress collection. Her knitwear has also been included in many group exhibitions – among them, 'Unravel: Knitwear in Fashion' in Antwerp (Belgium) and Enschede (the Netherlands) in 2011–12. Along with her design and consultancy work Iben also lectures at the Royal Danish Academy of Fine Arts, Schools of Architecture, Design and Conservation.

**What inspires and influences your designs?**
I am fascinated by the creation of three-dimensional shapes and forms. Choosing the yarn, developing new stitches and creating shapes that can be utilized in garment form is amazing. I am inspired by the traditional craft elements of making knitwear and my approach is very hands-on. I relate all my designs to the body, working directly with the knitted textures on the human form.

The architectural beauty of the natural world – botanical forms and structures found in plants, shells, flowers and seed-heads, gossamer insect wings and feathers – also inspires me. I live and work close to the sea and forest and always collect things when outside. I treasure antique and handcrafted textiles, having a deep appreciation of the effort, time and love that has gone into handworked garments. I try to evoke the same kind of feeling when creating my designs.

**Can you describe your design process in a few sentences?**
My design process is very instinctive; I do not have a plan, but generally follow where my ideas take me. I work exclusively with Italian spinners and rely solely on my intuition to select colours and yarns. At the same time I work on stitch concepts, sometimes working from previous developments and taking them forward.

This is play time, where things might happen by mistake, or something develops, and I realize it has immense potential – this is the best part of the working process. Once I have my stitch ideas I work with larger panels and drape directly onto the stand, trying out ways of using the stitches and the shapes or patterns they form. I photograph ideas along the way. Shapes are sketched out and then the collection is edited into a concise line of about 20 styles.

**What types of machine are used in the production of your work?**
I work on a 12-gauge old-fashioned industrial Stoll hand-driven machine and 7-, 5- and 3-gauge domestic hand-flat machines. Due to the combination of fully fashioned and hand-manipulated stitch work, my designs cannot be produced on computer machines. It is the hands and head of the knitter that create, not the machine itself.

**What techniques do you apply to your work?**
I use many techniques, but love the huge scope of partial knitting. For my more ethereal and gossamer constructions I explore drop-stitch effects in combination with partial knitting. I work with techniques simultaneously, knitting the actual piece and never adding anything after the process – no embellishment and no 'cheating'.

**What makes a successful knitwear designer?**
Creating your own handwriting, surprising people and making something real women want to wear.

**What advice would you give to someone who is considering setting up their own knitwear business?**
Only do it if you absolutely must, and if you must – love every minute of it!

**Top:** Piece by Iben Høj created on a domestic hand-flat knitting machine, working freely using drop stitch and hand-transfer effects together with partial knitting.

**Bottom:** Close-up detailing of a piece by Iben Høj, illustrating the organic structured knit worked quite freely by knitting and then putting it back onto the machine in different directions, like painting/patchworking with the textile structure.

## Insertions

Add interest to your knitting by adding insertions, which can be created by applying additional shapes to a knitted background. This is a time-consuming procedure, but the results can be impressive. Triangles, flaps, knots, plaited tube knitting, frills and ruffles can be knitted in advance and then incorporated into your knitting while it is being worked, or applied onto the knitted surface after completion. For example, the machine-knitted lace sample opposite has been made using a silk slub yarn and incorporating a decorative vintage lace trim into the knitted fabric while working it by hooking the trim onto the needle bed and then knitting, adding delicacy to the fabric.

If adding an insertion, knit the shape(s) to the required size and then knit onto a piece of waste yarn for several rows, then run off the machine or needles. You can then press the knitted insertions or shapes and add them into the knitting onto selected needles, making sure not to twist the stitches. The waste yarn is then unravelled down and removed from the knitting, leaving the insertions ready to be grafted into the knitting during the knitting process. The waste yarn should be a smooth yarn and contrasting in colour to the main knitting, making it easy to unravel and graft the knitted insertion into the knitting where required. Ruffles, commercially manufactured lace trimmings and braids can be picked up using the same technique.

Combining these techniques enables you to draw attention to particular areas of a garment. Full instructions can be found in any machine-knitting manual or any technical machine-knitting book.

**Below:** Metallic discs attached into the knitting by hooking each disc individually onto the stitch and placing back onto the needle, by Carol Brown.

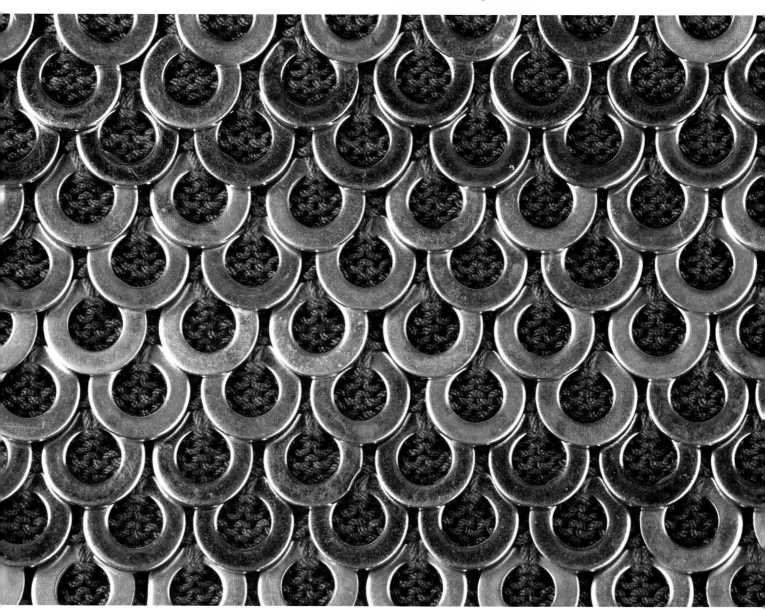

## Weaving

Weaving is a technique in which the needles pull an additional yarn through into the work while knitting. The simplest method of weaving on a knitting machine is to employ a punch-card design using the weaving brushes. This method has the advantage of having the right side of the fabric facing you while working, thereby making it far easier to create and develop your ideas, experimenting as you go. Highly textured yarns such as bouclé, mohair and ribbon can be woven in, adding textural qualities and surface structure to the design of the fabric.

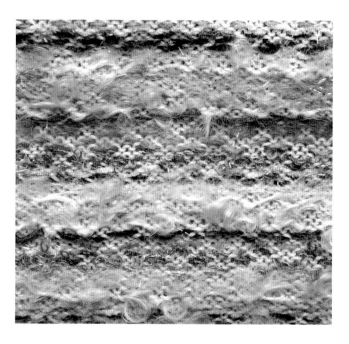

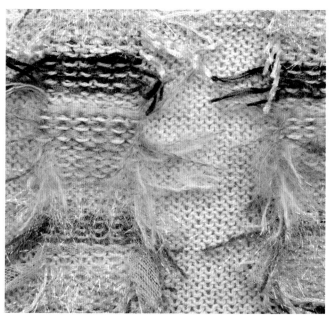

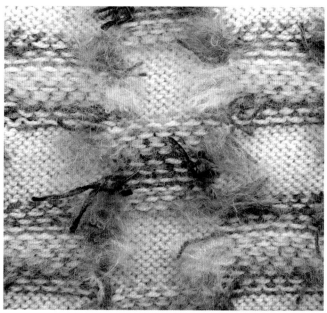

**Above left:** Knit weave sample, laying in the yarns, using a range of soft, muted colours in a range of textured yarns including mohair, silk slub, chenille, bouclé and ribbon yarns.

**Above right:** Punch-card woven panels with cut floats using highly textured yarns help secure the woven yarn and add stability to the fabric.

**Right:** Felted sample of knit weave with cut floats using pure wool, mohair and fine wool blend, producing a soft, distressed finish due to the milling process.

Weaving can also be worked manually by laying the selected weaving yarn across the knitting needles and knitting in. Very textured yarns work particularly well, being gripped into position by the holding stitches, which act as anchors by securing the yarn and providing greater stability in the fabric design. When using a punch card, long floats can often be seen. To add further texture these can be cut to give the surface a sumptuous fringed effect.

**Below:** 'Wrap Me Up, Protect Me' by Elizabeth Dyson – cocooning patchwork knits in soft textures and mohair yarns.

## Pleats

Pleating fabric gives greater fullness and, as seen here, various pleat designs can be formed by careful needle selection when knitting, including knife, accordion and box pleats.

Knitted pleats are worked into the fabric by varying the tension and knitting tight and loose rows, thus creating a fold line in the fabric. Young London-based Korean designer Hanjoo Kim demonstrates the creativity that can be achieved with the technique of pleating, adding both structure and movement to the fabric (see opposite).

A range of pleated structures designed in paper by Helena Rees to explore a variety of ideas, and used to create a range of garments with pleating as the focus point.

Sleeve detailing by Hanjoo Kim combining jacquard and pleats.

# SURFACE MANIPULATION

Surface decoration applied to knitwear is an easy and versatile way of producing individual garments. There are many different ways of doing this, including embroidery, tassels, beadwork and fringing – both alone or in combination. Decorating the surface of a simple garment is an ideal technique for beginners; it allows you to concentrate on learning the basics and focus on knitting the basic shape of the garment, rather than having to concentrate on complicated patterns and colour work.

For the experienced knitter or knitwear designer, surface decoration is not only an important fashion feature, but a style of knitting that explores colour and design, combining complicated knitted structures with decorative surface textile work.

**Opposite top:** Drawing and planning out the embroidery and embellishment of a garment design by Hannah Risdon.

**Right:** Black knitted, hooded dress appliquéd with silver doily embellishment with net under-skirting by Alexander McQueen.

## Embroidery and surface decoration

Embroidery is a medium for decorating textile surfaces, with knitting providing the perfect canvas area. Usually the most successful results are achieved on a garment with a relatively simple shape that is knitted in a stitch to create a smooth, flat surface area to work upon. A personal touch can be added to a shop-bought knitted garment by adding embroidery to highlight a seam or enhance a border design. For beginners, a dropped-sleeve, slashed-neck sweater or any similar-shaped garment can be transformed into an inspirational, individual design by embroidering stitches in well-selected contrasting or complementary colours around the neckline, hem or cuffs, or on a pocket. For the more advanced knitter, embroidery can be used to highlight a design that needs only a small amount of colour to highlight and strengthen a motif, picture knit or design feature – on a pocket top or yoke, for example.

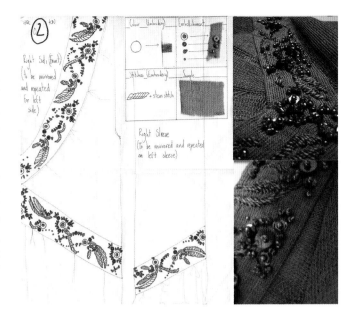

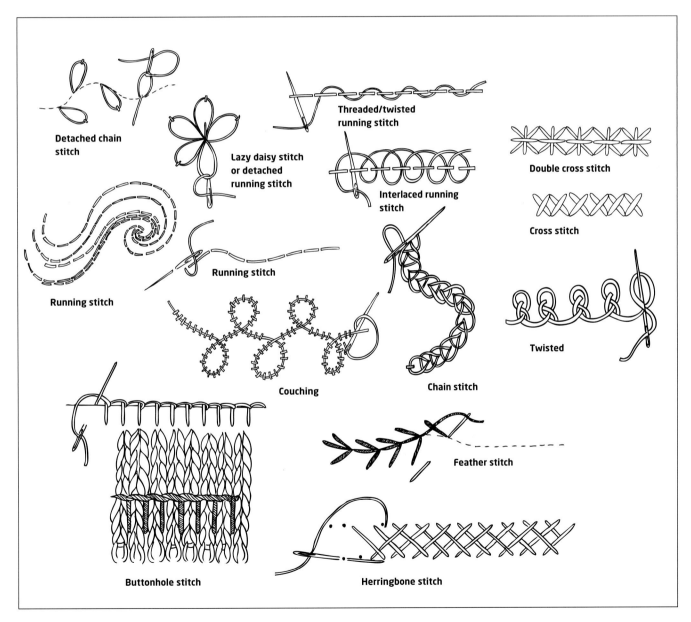

**Detached chain stitch**

**Lazy daisy stitch or detached running stitch**

**Threaded/twisted running stitch**

**Interlaced running stitch**

**Double cross stitch**

**Cross stitch**

**Running stitch**

**Running stitch**

**Couching**

**Chain stitch**

**Twisted**

**Buttonhole stitch**

**Feather stitch**

**Herringbone stitch**

Embroidery can be used in knitwear to:

◆ Add colour

◆ Add texture

◆ Emphasize a particular stitch or design

◆ Work in a small amount of colour to highlight a design

◆ Highlight a seam or design feature on a garment, neckline or button stand.

Embroidery has been used through the ages to decorate and enhance knitwear. Victorians embellished their work with combinations of cross-stitch embroidery and intricate Swiss darning, typical of the elaborate and ornate dress of this era. In the latter half of the twentieth century fashions in knitwear changed radically, from the commercial emphasis of the 1970s to the hand-knitted garments of the 80s and the technological development of seamless knitting of the 90s. Today individualistic designs by cutting-edge designers push the boundaries of technology in three-dimensional knitted surfaces, along with the development of smart textiles.

**Above:** Highly decorative embroidered and embellished hand- and machine-knit samples by mixed media textile artist Sue Bradley, who specializes in knitted and embroidered fabrics for interiors, fashion and textile art.

**Below:** Sketch out designs for embroidery of East European textile art.

When developing ideas for decorating and embroidering garments, it is useful to research your ideas thoroughly. Possible sources of inspiration include all types of textile books, both historical and contemporary. European and Far Eastern costume books, in particular, will help you to appreciate colour combinations and contrasts and allow you to interpret ideas from simple motifs to repeat designs. The following embroidery stitches work especially well when used as a decorative finish: chain stitch, cross stitch, French knots, blanket stitch (particularly for edgings and on hemlines), lazy daisy stitch, stem stitch and Swiss darning. Any of these stitches can be used alone or worked in conjunction with one another. All the listed stitches can be found in any good embroidery book.

For embroidering knitwear, special embroidery yarns can be purchased in a wide range of shades, but these do tend to be expensive. An alternative is to use small oddments of yarn, ranging from smooth to slub yarns, depending on whether you want to add further texture to your design. Don't limit your samples to the most widely used or available materials. Rich surface textures can be achieved by working into the surface texture, using all sorts of yarns, threads, tapes and ribbons.

Experiment by knitting a 15cm square in the appropriate stitch for your garment and by working into the surface area. Wash the sample as you would the finished garment, to check that the yarns blend well.

**Top right:** Swiss darning, also known as 'duplicate stitch', is the embroidery technique that is worked by tracing over the knitted stitch and can be used to add small amounts of colour to a design.

**Right:** Horizontal machine-knitted stripe sample decorated with hand-embroidered chain stitch circles worked into the surface fabric.

**Below:** Experimental, free-form embroidery samples by Hungarian fashion designer Dora Keleman, manipulating the surface structure through knit, embroidery, stitching and distressing the fabric.

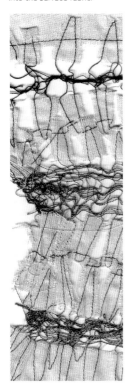
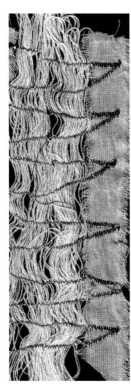
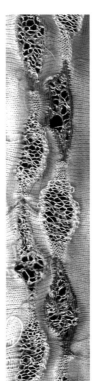
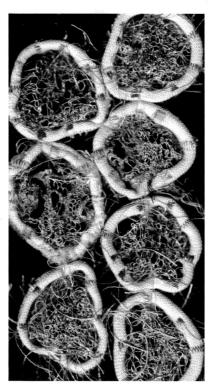
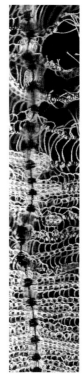

**Right:** Strong, bright, bold, abstract embroidery embellishes the work of British designer Claire Tough.

**Below:** Colourful, abstract, graffiti-inspired patchwork, embroidered knitwear by Clare Tough, Autumn/Winter 2007/08.

**Above:** An innovative patchwork of design by British designer Jenny Postle that challenges our concept of knitwear and explores colour, texture, and surface structure for Autumn/Winter 2011/12.

**Left:** Highly embellished embroidered knitwear by Claire Tough inspired by urban influences, graffiti and the Hip Hop scene of the '80s.

## Bead embroidery

There are two main methods of attaching beads and sequins to a garment. The first and easiest method is to position the beads or trims on the finished garment and then sew them on individually. Positioning the individual beads with the completed section of knitting in front of you like this enables you to experiment with the bead embroidery design without affecting your knitting pattern. When adding beads or any other attachments to knit always remember that the knitted fabric must be strong enough to hold them in position and not distort under their weight.

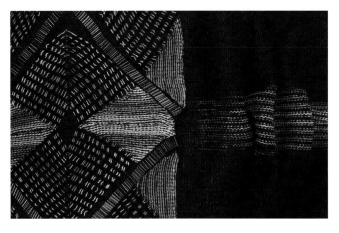

**Above:** 'Bedazzled' by Hannah Swainson.

**Below:** Highly embellished knitted textile collection 2011 by Florence Spurling, combining both hand and machine techniques with great attention to detail.

The second method is to incorporate the beads or sequins into your knitting while you work. In essence this is also a relatively simple method, but it can be time consuming and fiddly. When working this method, take a stitch off the needle and thread the bead onto it. Transfer the beaded stitch back onto the needle and continue to knit. Whole designs can be created in this fashion, introducing complicated beadwork designs or smaller sections where the beads and sequins are used to highlight and introduce further colour, texture and interest to the design.

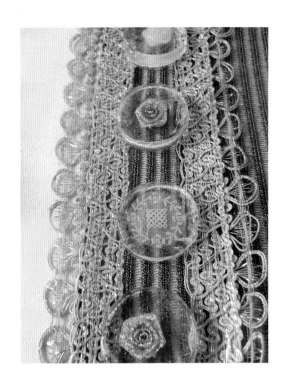

**Below:** Simple stripes of knitting by Carol Brown, using a variety of natural yarns, including pure silk, cotton slubs and wool bouclé to create a textured fabric, embellished with mother of pearl buttons in an assortment of shapes and sizes.

**Right:** Highly embellished knit sample with decorative braid and resin buttons by Lauren Fenn.

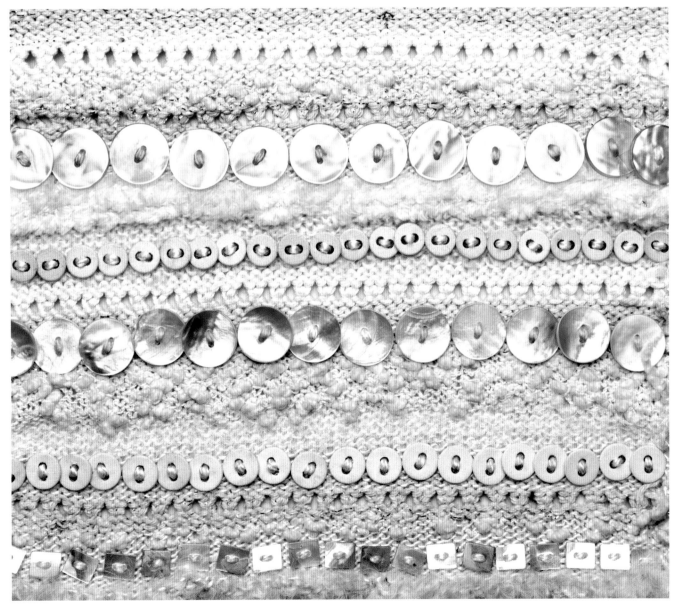

## Decorative applied tube knitting

Tube knitting (also known as 'rouleau knitting') is a narrow strip of knitting that resembles French knitting, worked over three or four needles of the machine bed. Using the main tension dial to cast on with the appropriate yarn thickness, knit four rows holding the knitting firmly down or hang on a claw weight. Set the machine to knit in one direction only and knit to the required length. As you knit, the row that slips will pull the yarn across the knitting, making the edges curl together to form a tube, hence the name. The length of tube knitting can then be sewn onto a garment, adding pattern, colour and texture. Tube knitting can also be used as an insertion, a garment drawstring or an edging. The piece below has been produced by knitting lengths of tube knitting and then shaping and stitching them into flower motifs, which could be applied to a garment as a corsage or trim or stitched together to form a new piece of fabric. Tube knitting can also be plaited or woven into lace knitting.

**Opposite top:** Bespoke knitwear designs by British designer Rosalind Price Cousins, including an ostrich knit and feather neck ruff, machine-knit neck and fringed cuff accessories, 'lyrebird'-inspired neckpiece, using a range of luxurious yarns.

**Opposite below:** Fringe knitting being worked on a domestic knitting machine.

Beaded and embroidered tube-knitted sculptured flower fabric from the 'Breeze' collection 2011 by Carol Brown.

## Tassels

Tassels are easy to make from lengths of cut yarn. Bunch the lengths together and double them over. Tie a knot at the top of the loop, which will then hold all the yarn lengths in place, and then bind the tassel 15mm from the top. Finish the binding by sewing the yarn under the binding and bringing the needle out at the top, then stitch neatly to secure. Tassels can be as simple or elaborate as your design requires.

## Fringing

Fringing can be produced by machine or by hand. Manually produced fringing is very easy to make and is similar in technique to tassels. Cut your yarn into strands double the length of the finished tassel. Taking several strands to the thickness of the required tassel, fold over the yarn lengths and then, using a crochet hook, pull the strands of yarn through the knitting before hooking the yarn lengths up through the tassel loop to secure the tassel. Continue this process across a knitted edge to produce a thick fringed edging, which can be used to trim a hem or edging. Fringing can be enhanced by combining it with beadwork, sequins, embroidery or knotting effects, depending on your individual design.

# 4
## INNOVATIVE TECHNIQUES

This chapter encourages freer consideration of the knit process – investigating and experimenting with fabric development by combining techniques and working with new yarns and materials. It reflects on the use of traditional and non-traditional practices and new knit technologies to create exciting and innovative designs that bear little resemblance to our previous perceptions of knitting.

In recent years, knitwear has seen a rebirth as a medium used in fashion, product design, furniture, interiors and fine art. Through the application and investigation of new techniques and materials, such as plastics, metal, rubber and resin, knitting has been revolutionized, resulting in greater recognition. The craft has grown in popularity, with many contemporary, cutting-edge fashion and knit designers employing the medium and process of knitting, from the innovative designs of Issey Miyake, Yoshiki Hishinuma and Yohji Yamamoto to the 'extreme knitting' of Dutch designer Christien Meindertsma and the sculptural approach of the influential Swedish designer Sandra Backlund.

**Previous spread:** Knitting in progress – a patchwork of knitted shapes, sewn together to create a 'Giant Rug' by Christien Meindertsma, for the exhibition 'Design for a Living World', Cooper-Hewitt National Design Museum, New York.

**Left:** Red and white striped expressionist knit dress using industrial barrier tape by Craig Lawrence, Spring/Summer 2010 collection.

**Above:** 'Giant Rug' detail; each individual shape was made from 1.6kg of wool, the yield of a single sheep, sourced from a sustainable sheep ranch in Idaho.

# EXAGGERATED SCALE

Given the range of various types and gauges of knitting machine, from fine to very bulky, and also the hand-knitting needles available, many knit practitioners have started to experiment and create supersize knitted garments with irregular surface structures that envelop the body in voluminous, cocoon shapes. These extreme silhouettes are often worked fluently on large needles and fashioned organically by twisting and shaping the knitting to create interesting and new structures.

Scale and structure can be worked through clever use of yarn selection – for example, volume can be created either by using chunky, heavyweight yarns or by combining many strands of yarn together. Contrast can then be added by juxtaposition with the finest of yarns. Many of these supersize garments are created spontaneously and progressively, shaping the structure of the knitting as worked rather than being pre-planned, and exploring yarn weights and combining more than one stitch structure to emphasize the yarns' properties, scale and proportion.

Highly textured chunky knitwear by Taiwanese designer Johan Ku, from his 2011 'The Hole' collection.

## CASE STUDY
# SANDRA BACKLUND

Sandra Backlund is a contemporary Swedish knitwear designer. She studied knitwear design in Stockholm and graduated in 2004. In the same year she founded her own label. Sandra has quickly become an influential name in the world of knitting. She is renowned for her complex knitted structures, which are sculpted and created around the body. Her work investigates shape and form, distorting and exaggerating the natural outline of the body in an exploration of scale, producing strong silhouettes. Her previous collections include 'Control-C', 'Last Breath Bruises' and 'Body, Skin and Hair'.

An excellent knowledge of traditional knit techniques underpins Sandra's work, giving her the freedom to work fluently when modelling and sculpting her garments three-dimensionally on the stand or the body – a conceptual approach that has inspired many young designers in turn. Sandra works freely, knitting and constructing new shapes, through exploration of technique, building up the silhouette, testing and trying out new ideas, and experimenting with detail until the garment is formed. Her work is regularly selected by editors to feature in magazines internationally, and she has also exhibited worldwide.

**What is the concept behind your label?**
I like to think of fashion as an expression of art, rather than an industry. A democratic form of art that most of us do relate to in our everyday life. People in general could of course be more self-governed when it comes to fashion, but even if you don't think about it or actually care about it, the choices you make about what you wear are still an expression of something. It can be a personal or political statement, a way to become someone else or to blend in and look like everyone else, or just for aesthetic reasons.

**Who or what have been your biggest inspirations artistically?**
Apart from the handicraft techniques and the materials I work with, I'm really fascinated by all the ways you can highlight, distort and transform the natural silhouette of the human body with clothes and accessories. I like to consciously dress and undress parts of the body. I'm really introverted and lock myself in my studio when working, so I guess I find inspiration from everything that is going on in my life, both private and professionally.

**Can you describe your design process in a few sentences?**
With the human body as the main starting point I improvise on a tailor's dummy or on my own body to discover ideas for shapes and silhouettes that I could never come up with in my head. I allow myself to lose control and see what happens if I don't think so much about practical things and what others might expect from me. I don't sketch; instead I work with a three-dimensional collage method where I develop some basic blocks that I multiply and attach to each other until they become a garment. Then one thing leads to another and in the end the collection is almost like a personal mind map.

**You produce garments and collections; do you get involved with other projects?**
Not really, everything I do right now is about fashion one way or another.

**What is the key to your success?**
Instead of concentrating too much on living up to the image of being a new fashion designer, I am actually working as one.

**What is your greatest achievement to date?**
The fact that both I and my company are still alive after seven years of extremely hard work.

**What was the most difficult challenge in establishing your own business?**
Keeping the creative freedom and still finding ways to support myself.

**What advice would you give to someone who is considering setting up their own knitwear business?**

In the beginning it's important to spend a lot of time experimenting on your own to find what is special about you and what you're good at. One way to do this is to explore the basics and be aware of any mistakes and ideas along the way that can take you beyond what you knew before.

**What is your future vision for your work?**

My plan is to continue to work hard, protect my origins and what I am good at, but still find ways to develop my designs and my company. I am a searcher so I will never find myself reaching some kind of finishing line, but I would, of course, like to be able to live off my work.

Sculptured knit 'Control-C' collection 2009/10 by Sandra Backlund with emphasis on shape and structure, exaggerating the body silhouette.

# THREE-DIMENSIONAL KNITTING

Many designers take a conceptual approach to their work, manipulating and transforming the knitted structure into three-dimensional forms. Designers, such as Sandra Backlund and Kim Choong-Wilkins are recognized for their exploration of the body, applying extreme shapes that exaggerate and distort the natural body form and push the boundaries of the design capabilities of knitting.

Knitting lends itself to sculptural shaping, either by fibre choice or by creating a three-dimensional structure through the use of technology. Sculptural forms that mould to and distort the body can be created through the application of either single or combined techniques, which include building up the knitted structure, layering knit upon knit, moulding the knit and applying innovative pattern-cutting techniques, as discussed in Chapter 5 (see pp.166ff.).

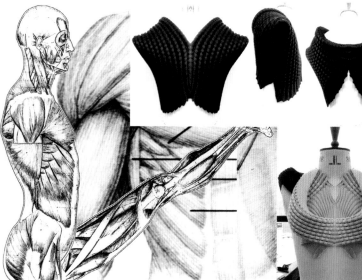

'Bodybound' menswear collection by innovative designer Kim Choong-Wilkins, inspired by research, images, anatomical sketches, design developments and modelling fabric on the stand.

**Right:** Design detail from the menswear collection 'Bodybound', created by Kim Choong-Wilkins and inspired by skin, sinew, muscle and bone, and the macabre photography of Joel-Peter Witkin.

**Below:** From the same 'Bodybound' collection, designs featuring dramatic detailing, statement spikes and fabric contrasts.

## BUILDING UP THE KNITTED STRUCTURE

Build up the knitted structure by applying various knitting techniques such as short-row or partial knitting, or moulding and sculpting knitting to the shape required, as illustrated in Chapter 3.

Innovative three-dimensional structures can also be created by applying additional shapes onto a knitted background. This is a time-consuming process, but the results can be impressive. Triangles, flaps, knots, plaited tube knitting, frills and ruffles can be knitted in advance and then incorporated into the knitting while it is being worked or applied onto the knitted surface after completion.

Experiment by sculpting the fabric into three-dimensional forms by adding volume through draping, pleating and gathering. Consider contrasting chunky-weight with fine-gauge yarns, and exploiting the physical characteristics of the fibre – for example by working with elasticized yarns with excellent stretch properties that add shape and structure, offer support and mould the garment to the figure. There are many elasticated yarns on the market that are perfect for either knitting in with another yarn or for embellishing the knitted surface.

**Opposite page top:** Decorative neck and bodice accessory ' Second Skin', by Australian designer Alana Clifton-Cunningham, 2007.

**Opposite page bottom:** Detail of 'Second Skin' in pure wool and Tasmanian oak.

**Right:** Intricate textured bobble and cable sleeveless polo-neck vest, inspired by tribal and body scarification, combining both traditional and contemporary techniques, by Alana Clifton-Cunningham.

**Below:** Close-up detailing of the same bobble and cable design.

Consider layering knit upon knit or knit on woven fabric or using other materials to build up volume through skilful pattern shaping. Layers can be knitted and attached manually or on the knitting machine.

Three-dimensional techniques can also be created with the working application of shibori (see pp. 155–56) and other expert treatments, such as felting, moulding and laser cutting the knitted fabric.

As explained in Chapter 2, sampling plays an important role in developing and challenging a technique, enabling you to explore various processes, and resulting in new and innovative ideas. Sampling a technique can be time consuming. However, you will find that your work gains a greater sophistication through the handling of the yarn, fabrics or materials you are exploring and by testing out new ideas, which is all part of the design development process. Always look closely at the process, making notes of the various stages and results for future reference.

**Below left:** Industrially knitted fabric by Elana Adler, a graduate of Rhode Island School of Design, US.

**Below right:** Industrially knitted and hand-cut fabric by Elana Adler, whose ideas are expressed 'through colour, texture, pattern and shape'.

**Right:** Industrially knitted cut fabric by Elana Adler.

# KNIT AND WOVEN COMBINED

Knit and woven fabrics can be combined together in one garment to produce contrasts in fabric weight, handle and texture, adding interesting juxtapositions: a large-scale soft tweed fabric worked with a lace-weight 100 per cent linen yarn, for example; a bronze metallic-finish suede worked with a knitted silk slub yarn; or a soft, sculptured traditional cable fabric combined with leather, suede or rubber.

In contrast to woven fabric, knit offers great elasticity. Fabrics do, however, need to be selected carefully to work with each other successfully, as technical problems may arise. One fabric may react with the other during the manufacture of the garment, pulling and distorting it or distorting the garment seams. It may also be difficult to wash the garment if one fabric shrinks more than the other.

**Below:** Figure-hugging knit dress with circular fabric insertions in sleeve and skirt design by London-based, Canadian designer Mark Fast, Spring/Summer 2010.

**Right:** Body-conscious, fitted bodice and fitted leggings with ladder-lace detailing in knit and woven by Mark Fast, Spring/Summer 2010.

**Below right:** Dress in knit and woven fabric – ready-to-wear collection by Ohne Titel, Autumn/Winter 2010/11.

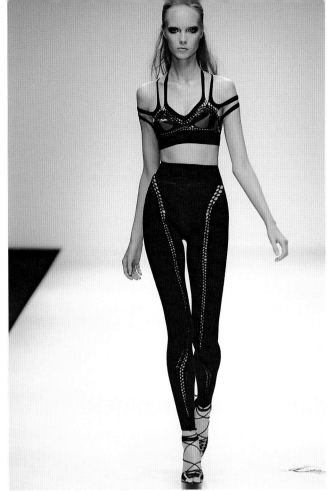

**Left:** Futuristic 'translucent puffy jacket' in knit and woven fabrics by Hungarian designer Dora Kelemen, 2009.

**Below:** Fine, transparent ribbed knit and woven fabric combine and contrast, by Dora Kelemen, 2009.

# MERGING CRAFT AND TECHNOLOGY

Inventive fabrics can be created through fusing craft and technology, merging traditional and non-traditional techniques to transform the fabric into something new. It is also possible to experiment with both traditional and contemporary techniques, such as working cables with laser-cut fabric to create bespoke designs. As seen on the international catwalks, many contemporary designers are now working with laser cutting, producing intricate cut-outs from the fabric in complex designs, working freely to challenge the medium and merge technology with fine craftsmanship.

**Below:** Three-dimensional textured, structured knit in merino wool and polyamide by Austrian designer Veronika Persché.

**Right:** 'Pocketerle' three-dimensional design with transparent pockets containing paperclips, producing a decorative fabric by Veronika Persché.

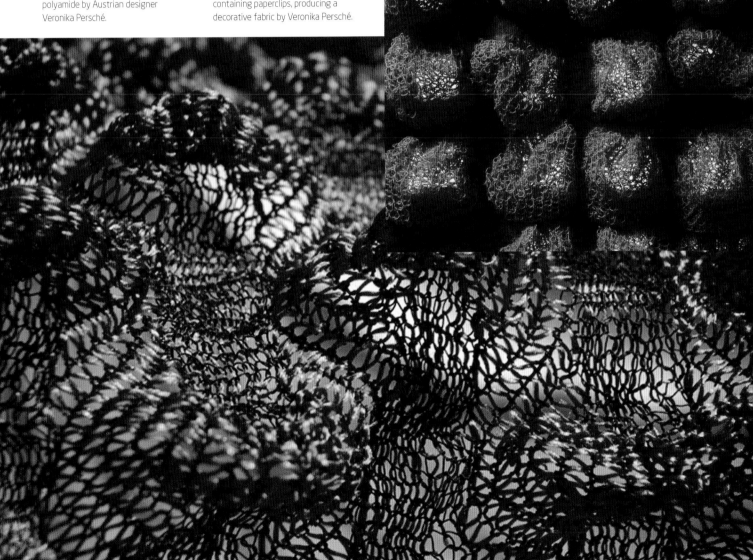

There are many different techniques you can try. Experiment with layering knit on knit, using fine knitted fabric or other materials and then stitching through the layers; working into the surface and manipulating the surface texture; burning the fabric; cutting into the layers leaving raw and distressed surface detailing; trapping items of interest into the knitting, like the work of Veronika Persché (see pp.26–27, 149).

There are many innovative yarns on the market, including steel and light-reflective yarns, metal threads, elastics and washable paper yarns, rubbers and latex. All of these are worth experimenting with so that you gain a greater understanding of their individual properties and can use them to add new dimensions to your work. Knitting with steel yarns makes for interesting results. The steel yarns used for knitting are usually produced bound in wool or with a silk core, making the yarn pliable and easy to manipulate, and offering sculptural characteristics, a softer finish and flexibility.

Many knitwear designers have a multidisciplinary approach to their work, straddling several different areas and using mixed-media applications and experimentation with various knit finishes to transform their fabrics into something new and unique. Dynamic visual effects can be achieved by boiling, bleaching, ageing, foiling, distressing and brushing to create tactile and interesting finishes. Experiment with natural and synthetics fibres. Play with the tension of structures, proportion and scale. Consider knitting samples and then working into and onto the surface fabric using screen printing, digital printing and resist dye techniques to add further interest and explore the potential of your fabric.

**Bottom left:** Detail from the 'Peony jacket' by Alison Waite, knitted in seven pieces on a Shima WG Accessory machine, a flexible machine able to shape and produce integral knitting with no cutting and no waste during the production process.

**Below:** Back view of the jacket.

**Right:** Full view of the jacket.

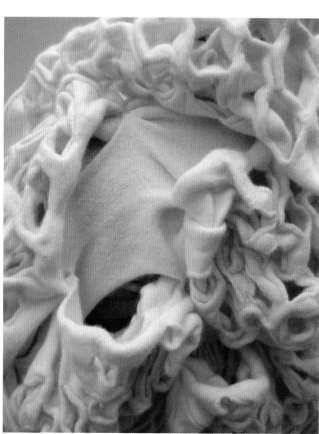

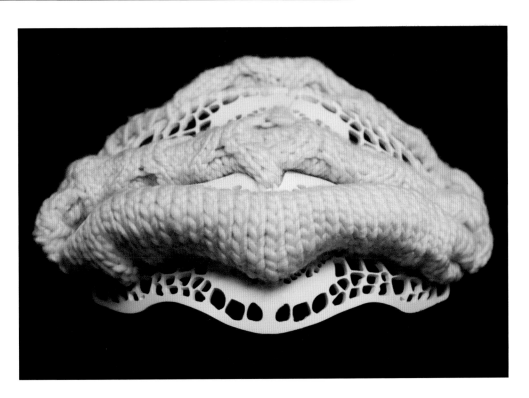

**Left:** Innovative fusion between traditional and modern techniques are combined in the designs of Jessica Hope Medlock, using textural relief knitting in wool and acrylic mix with three-dimensional laser-cut acrylic.

**Below:** Laser-cut acrylic combined with heavily textured cable knitting, by Jessica Hope Medlock.

CASE STUDY

# DEREK LAWLOR

Contemporary British designer Derek Lawlor graduated from Central Saint Martins with an MA in Fashion Knitwear. He expanded his training by working with designers such as Michiko Koshino, V. V. Rouleaux and Jasper Gardiva, and launched his first collection on the catwalk at London's Graduate Fashion Week, to great acclaim. In Autumn/Winter 2010 he designed a stunning capsule collection in collaboration with Marimekko, the leading Finnish textile and clothing design company, which captured and interpreted the Marimekko patterns and expressed their unique style.

Derek has received excellent press coverage from Vogue.com, Dazed.com, *Grazia*, *Elle* and many other international publications. His work is bold, innovative and expressive in both silhouette and form. His designs use contrasting materials, from the traditional to non-traditional, and he is experimental in his approach, challenging the physical properties and characteristics of materials and techniques and then applying them to his work with effortless fluidity.

Lawlor has a first-rate understanding of fabric development, which he translates into sculptural garments. His lacing technique is original, adding impact to his work, and giving a flowing, organic but contemporary edge. His creations straddle the boundaries between 'artwork and fashion, craft and performance, commanding attention in their complexity'. Collaborative projects have included working with dancers from the Royal Ballet School, with stylist/art director Olivia Pomp and photographer Rick Guest, in unique forms of the presentation of his work.

**How did you get into knitwear design?**
I always knew I wanted to work in fashion. During my degree I specialized in knit and weave, but I wasn't interested in just creating fabrics; I wanted to take my work to the next level, experimenting with my fabrics on the body.

**When and why did you start your own business?**
After presenting my first collection after graduation I got some really good press, and I was approached about producing further work – it just happened. It's been great!

**What is the concept behind your label?**
It's all about the fabric; my work is technique-based, pushing the boundaries of knitting.

**Who or what have been your biggest inspirations artistically?**
There are lots of people who inspire me, and lots of people who have supported me and continue to support my work.

**What is the most difficult part of designing a collection?**
The most difficult part of my work is keeping everything running smoothly. While designing a new collection I am completing all the orders for the previous collection, alongside working on commissions and individual projects.

**Can you describe your design process?**
Research – visiting galleries/exhibitions and referring to my fashion/knitting archive for inspiration, then working directly on the knitting machine. My work is fabric first, and shape and silhouette second.

**Who was your first client?**
After launching my first collection I was invited by Kate Phelan into the offices of *Vogue*, London, to present my work, which was a great honour. It just went from there.

**What is the most enjoyable aspect of your work?**
The freedom to be creative.

**What is a typical working day in your life as a designer?**
Days are varied. I tend to answer emails and oversee the business in the morning, and work on the collections in the afternoon.

**What advice would you give an aspiring designer who wants to launch his or her own business?**
Work with designers, complete internships, gain as much experience as possible, and learn how the industry works from different perspectives.

**What is your ultimate goal for your label?**
The ultimate goal for my work is greater recognition internationally for the creativity of merging art and fashion, and, most importantly, to be true to myself.

**Top:** Heavily embellished knitwear design with manipulated cord detailing.

**Right:** Bespoke knitwear design, with cord detailing organically woven through the fabric, Autumn/Winter 2010.

# FELTING

Dramatic textural qualities can be worked by felting knit, which is achieved by washing in high temperatures either in a washing machine or by hand, while shaping, controlling or distorting the fabric. During the washing process the fibres of the yarn expand, shrinking the knit to create a compact, durable fabric, often with loss of the stitch definition. The initial results can be unpredictable and will vary depending on the type of yarn, the size of the piece of knitting or garment and the quantity of knit being felted at any one time. With experience and thorough testing, making notes as you work, you will be able to calculate the shrinkage of the knitted fabric. With careful monitoring the work can be controlled, resulting in visually stunning designs that are sensitive and refined in weight and handle. The tighter the tension of the knitted sample, the denser the fabric will be when felted. The looser the tension, the less compact and finer in handle it will be.

To give added textural effects, coins, shells, stones, marbles or any other similar objects can be wrapped and bound into the knit before felting. The felted fabric will mould itself around the objects; when the objects are removed after washing, the fabric maintains the objects' shape, producing fascinating three-dimensional tactile qualities and new design possibilities, as illustrated here in the work of Jeung-Hwa Park. Applying and exploring different methods of folding, pleating and twisting the fabric, and experimenting with the size and number of objects wrapped will enable you to manipulate and transform the fabric to achieve the desired effect.

Yarns that felt particularly well include pure wool yarns that have not been chemically treated, such as alpaca, lambswool and mohair. There are many yarns that are marketed especially for felting. When working with these, consider adding other non-felting yarns, such as slivers of metallic yarns, for added texture and surface sheen. Once a knit has been felted, it forms a fabric with a finished edge that does not fray. It can also be combined with other techniques, such as laser cutting, appliqué, embroidery and dyeing, all of which will add additional surface interest.

Exploration with felting knit could include:

◆ Playing with tension

◆ Wrapping and binding the knit before felting by folding, pleating, stitching, twisting and gathering

◆ Recycling knits

◆ Combining the technique with weave, jacquard, ladder knitting, pleating, smocking, shibori and embroidery.

**Right:** Three-dimensional sculptured fabrics, using shibori techniques by designer Jeung-Hwa Park.

Machine-knitted sample transformed into stunning three-dimensional sculptured fabric by resist dyeing and felting, using shibori techniques, by Korean designer Jeung-Hwa Park.

# PRINTING AND DYEING EFFECTS ON KNITTING

Yarns and finished knitting can be transformed through the application of dyeing and printing processes. Consider using treatments such as dip dyeing – either dyeing the yarn before it is knitted up, or the fabric once it has been knitted. Alternatively, add colour to the knitted surface by hand painting it using rollers and brushes, or spraying coatings onto the knit, crossing the boundaries between knitting and art. Always consider the colourfastness of the dye in relation to the fibre being dyed.

**Resist methods of printing**

Shibori is a Japanese term, which refers to the method of resist-dyeing fabric, including the process of tie-dyeing. A surface pattern is created by binding the fabric before dyeing. This can be done by folding the fabric regularly or irregularly, by twisting, stitching, pressing or crumpling. When dyed, the folded areas will resist the dye, producing remarkable effects and transforming the fabric. This technique is usually applied to woven fabric; however, it is worth experimenting with the potential of the knitted surface design and the effects that can be created.

**Below left:** Needle transfer, bleaching and embellishment using Swarovski crystals and sequins applied and worked into the fabric to explore the theme 'rough and dirty' surfaces, by Sundus Akhter.

**Below right:** Contemporary menswear by Sundus Akhter, inspired by all aspects of workwear, including coal mining. This work shows great attention to surface textures.

## DISTRESSING KNIT

You may want to consider distressing the surface texture of knit by rubbing it to create friction in the fibres. You can also achieve similar tactile qualities by burning, singeing, bleaching or melting the fibres. With experimentation fascinating results can be achieved. Consider, too, the technique of devoré. This involves painting or printing sulphuric acid onto the surface of the knitted fabric; those parts of the fabric are then burnt away, leaving a distressed appearance. Care should be taken when applying this technique, however, due to the harmful chemicals involved.

**Right:** Hand-cut layered knitted textiles 'Echoes' by Amy Hunt with a play on tone-on-tone, using viscose, Lurex and Grilon yarns.

**Below:** Cut, layered-knit fabrics 'Echoes' by Amy Hunt, produced by heat-pressing, incorporating Grilon yarns, which react to heat, causing the fabric to harden. This hardening prevents fraying during the cutting process.

## LUMINOUS FILAMENT YARNS

Revolutionary new yarns are constantly being researched and developed, from ethically-friendly to high-tech yarns with advanced finishing treatments. Glow-in-the-dark or luminous-filament yarns have been developed with light-absorbing properties, creating unique and innovative yarns. Designs shown at the 2012 Mercedes-Benz Fashion Week, Tokyo, included London-based Taiwanese designer Johan Ku's dramatic glow-in-the-dark Spring/Summer collection, 'The Two Faces'. His garments appeared white with shimmering, ethereal effects in the light and glowed blue and green in the dark. The garments were made by combining a blend of natural fibres, including linen and bamboo, with artificial fibres that were interwoven with luminous light filaments.

Luminous filament yarns add great impact to garments and accessories on a fashion level, but they are also used in other industries, such as interiors and product design, and employed in the safety industry to produce high-visibility garments and materials.

Taiwanese designer Johan Ku presented his 'glow in the dark' collection entitled 'The Two Faces', at Tokyo Fashion Week – Spring/Summer 2012.

 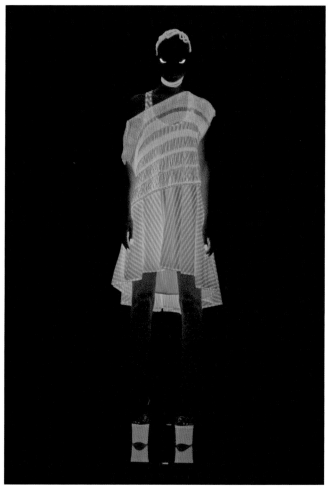

Three-dimensional knitted structure, created by Ginna Lee, a graduate of Central Saint Martins, whose work expresses 'visual manifestations of specific emotional moments or states'.

## CASE STUDY
# CRAIG LAWRENCE

One of London's bright new designers is Craig Lawrence, who was born in Ipswich, Suffolk, and studied fashion at Central Saint Martins, before gaining experience working for Gareth Pugh, and producing knitwear for his collections. He now has his own studio based in London.

Craig's work explores volume and structure, and his signature is innovative and experimental knitwear design. 'I design for anyone who's daring enough to wear my clothes', Craig says – a statement that is reflected in the list of celebrities who have worn his garments, which includes Lady Gaga, Tilda Swinton, Björk and Florence Welch.

He has been awarded the British Fashion Council's NEWGEN award for six seasons running. He has also had enviable support from the international press, including having had his work included in a special edition of *AnOther Magazine*, featuring Tilda Swinton wearing his design. Craig continues to work with Kate Shillingford, editor of *Dazed & Confused*, on knit and styling projects.

**What makes a successful knitwear designer?**
It's important to be inspired by a variety of things – unusual techniques and materials. Experimentation is key.

**What inspires and influences your designs?**
The atmosphere of places I visit, such as the seaside town Felixstowe, which is close to where I grew up. I also visit a DIY shop every season – I always find surprising inspiration there.

**What is the most difficult part of designing a collection?**
I tend to get carried away with experimenting with different yarns and techniques, so being able to edit down to make more of a cohesive collection is the biggest challenge.

**What types of machine are used in the design and production of your work?**
I do most of my knitting on domestic knit machines. We do some hand knits as well, and we'll be moving into some industrial factory production in the coming seasons.

**Can you describe your design process in a few sentences?**
I start with research images – these inform the yarns and colours for the collection. Then from this I experiment with different knit techniques that show off the yarn in the best way. I then pick swatches that I want to develop into the collection, and from there I start developing the silhouettes of the collection.

**How involved are you in the production processes?**
Because the process is organic all the samples are toiled and made in the studio.

**What are the advantages of setting up in business and working for yourself?**
You have a freedom to explore and grow at your own rate.

**What is your vision for your label?**
To always try and innovate knitwear by giving a different/fresh opinion. To never stay stagnant but always have an element of surprise. Doing pop-up shops and pop-up events would be a goal for the near future.

**What advice would you give an aspiring knitwear designer?**
You should research yarns and textures all the time. If you find something you like, buy it or take a photo because it may not be relevant at the time but can help as inspiration in the future. Be open-minded to things that you find scary.

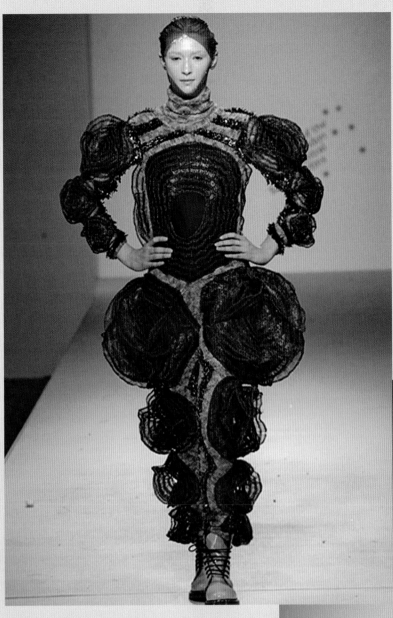

**Top:** Machine-knitted, sculptured purple dress designed by Craig Lawrence and inspired by tinsel and foil concertina Christmas decorations. It was worn by Björk at the Polar Music Prize in Sweden, 2010.

**Bottom:** Finely crafted full-length dress in spherical, moulded, laddered knit, sculptured around the body, by Craig Lawrence.

# SUSTAINABILITY

In recent years, there has been greater awareness of social and environmental issues and the interest in ethical fashion has grown as a result. This is partly due to increased media exposure and also to changes in attitudes to consumerism, with an increased awareness among the public, who are able to make informed decisions. With celebrity endorsements and support from models such as Laura Bailey, designers Stella McCartney and Wayne Hemingway, and broadcaster and naturalist David Attenborough, together with the birth of ethical fashion labels such as North Circular (an ethical fashion label established by model Lily Cole) acting as key driving forces, sustainability in fashion is creeping up the agenda.

The knitwear industry has been forced to react and designers are now working in collaboration with scientists and various professional associations to review and improve the recycling agenda. New developments have included the use of eco-friendly and biodegradable yarns, improved methods of dyeing and finishing, and greater improvements in machinery and manufacturing processes, and construction techniques, all of which are designed to work towards reducing the impact of the industry on the environment as a whole.

'Eco' collection comprising layered knits in a range of fabric weights by American designer Lauren Siegel, who was awarded the 'Rising Star Award at Vancouver Fashion Week 2010.

## UPCYCLING

Upcycling is the manufacture of something new from something old. It is the practice of renovating, improving and transforming unwanted things into something new and of better value. The queen of fun upcycling must be the free-spirited American designer Katwise, who first started creating colourful sweaters by recycling and reconstructing old knitwear finds, and found a market for these on her travels, making a very successful but fun business from her adventures. Many of her designs are created from patchworking, overlocking and stitching knitted garments together. Each design is unique and bears a name such as 'Elf Coat', 'Psychedelic Patchwork Rainbow Coat', 'Red Orange Fire Phoenix Coat' and 'Spellbound Coat'. Her garment range includes everything from dresses and coats to hoodies and hand and leg warmers, all produced by recycling and customizing knit.

Designer Sarah Ratty's eco outfit, produced under the eco-label 'Conscious Earthwear' in 1993 and made from recycled sweaters, is another excellent example of upcycling. In recent years there has also been a renewed interest in vintage fashion, make do and mend, recycling and remaking, customizing and transforming clothing, and producing versatile clothing that can be worn in more than one way.

Deconstructed garments have also made a popular return to the international catwalks, with many labels, including All Saints and Diesel, presenting their eco-conscious collections, which have attracted media attention and also made environmentally-friendly fashion available on the high street.

**Above:** Original upcycled knitted cream coat in a patchwork of overlocked cable, lace and ribbed knit panels by Katwise (Kat O'Sullivan).

**Right:** Knitwear by Makepiece, produced using natural yarns from sustainable farming and low-impact manufacture.

# SUSTAINABLE CLOTHING

Interest in sustainable clothing is growing within the fashion and textiles industry, with new developments in organic fabrics and yarn blends of the finest cashmere with long-fibre hemp, bamboo yarns and silk–hemp mixes, together with ethically produced recycled sari and silk yarns in a rich myriad of stunning colours.

Designer Professor Helen Storey, whose interests include new technologies linking the sciences and arts, has worked on several collaborative projects. With scientist Tony Ryan she worked on 'Winter Wonderland', investigating biodegradable fabrics, zero waste in the production cycle and low-impact manufacturing processes. She looked at how these can be applied in fashion with the aim of working towards a more sustainable future.

Studio Merel Karhof, a London-based product design studio, has crafted a wind-powered knitting machine (see opposite). The studio 'defines its work within public space and uses elements that people share, from the most obvious thing like the wind, to ignored details like the pattern on a manhole cover.' Many of their projects transcend product and question issues of sustainability, recycling, function and form.

The principles of the wind-powered knitting machine are simple: the aim is to harness and convert the energy produced by the motion of the wind into mechanical energy sufficient to power the machine. The machine knits from the outside towards the inside of the building, and then the knitting produced is 'harvested from time to time and rounded off into individually packaged scarves'. The time spent in the production of the scarf is identified on the label, making each individual item unique. If the wind is strong, the knitting machine will accelerate, increasing production. The weather dictates output, but the system is cost efficient and provides eco-friendly results.

All designers have their own signature approach to their work. Some designers focus on creating the fabric first, then sculpting it and draping it around the body. For other designers it is all about garment shape, structure and silhouette. By exploring various processes, combining techniques, reviewing the work of past designers, looking at cultural textiles and understanding yarn characteristics, you will be able to develop and invent new ideas of your own. Be aware of new developments in yarn and other materials; take note of what's happening in the arts, in the fashion, textile, design and manufacturing industries. When designing use your imagination, be creative with your ideas, explore and examine new techniques, combine the traditional with the new. Free your mind to fully examine all possibilities and the potential of knitting. There are no boundaries.

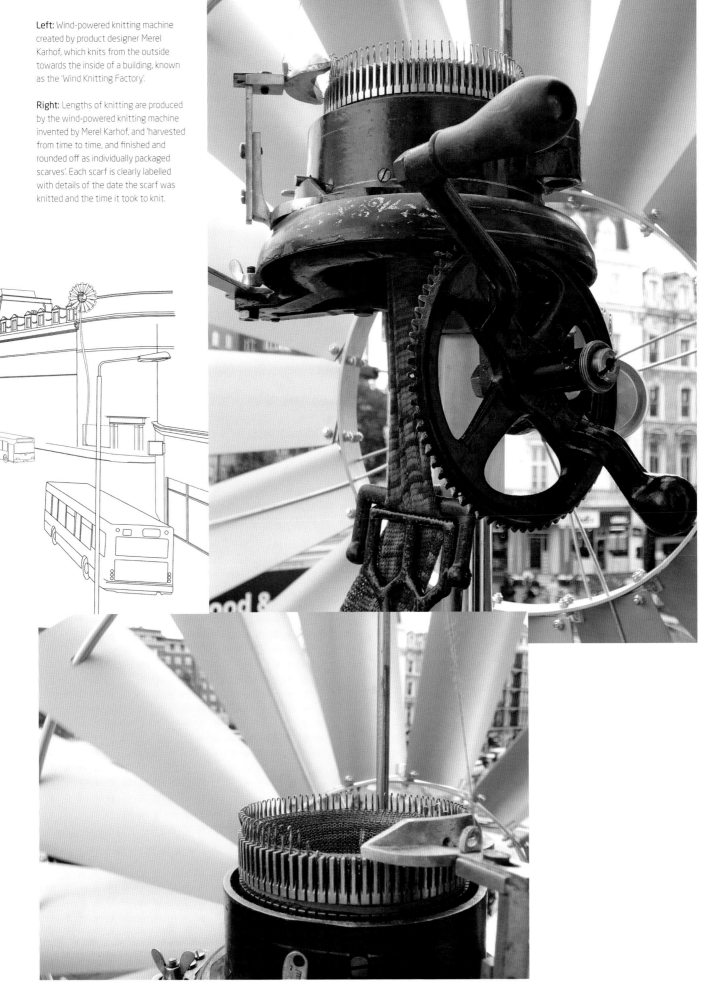

**Left:** Wind-powered knitting machine created by product designer Merel Karhof, which knits from the outside towards the inside of a building, known as the 'Wind Knitting Factory'.

**Right:** Lengths of knitting are produced by the wind-powered knitting machine invented by Merel Karhof, and 'harvested from time to time, and finished and rounded off as individually packaged scarves'. Each scarf is clearly labelled with details of the date the scarf was knitted and the time it took to knit.

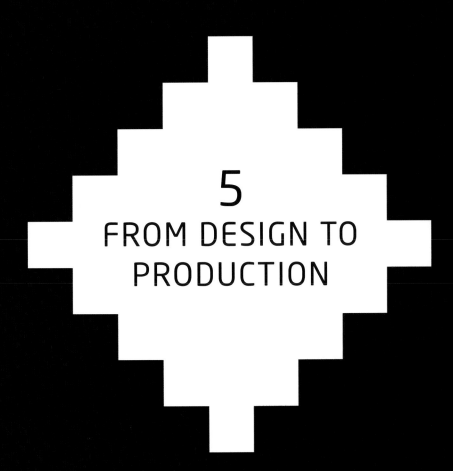

5

# FROM DESIGN TO PRODUCTION

How is a design produced? This chapter explains the stages involved, from creating and analysing your design, pattern drafting and pattern calculation through to garment production and finishing. There is a great deal of creativity involved in garment development and this chapter will show you how to cut a flat pattern and how to model on the stand to realize your design. Sound knowledge of the basics involved in graphing out a shape and the calculations required to draft a pattern will result in a good garment fit and provide you with the information required to construct and finish a successful garment or collection.

**Previous page:** 'Architectural Knits', produced by Stoll Trend Collection Spring/Summer 2013, which focus on the influence of architecture in knits. The piece shown is fashioned in double jersey and explores feature edges, pleats, folding and plissé effects, reflecting the extensive spectrum of knitting technologies.

**Below:** Ideas board by Na'ama Rietti, exploring both structure and form.

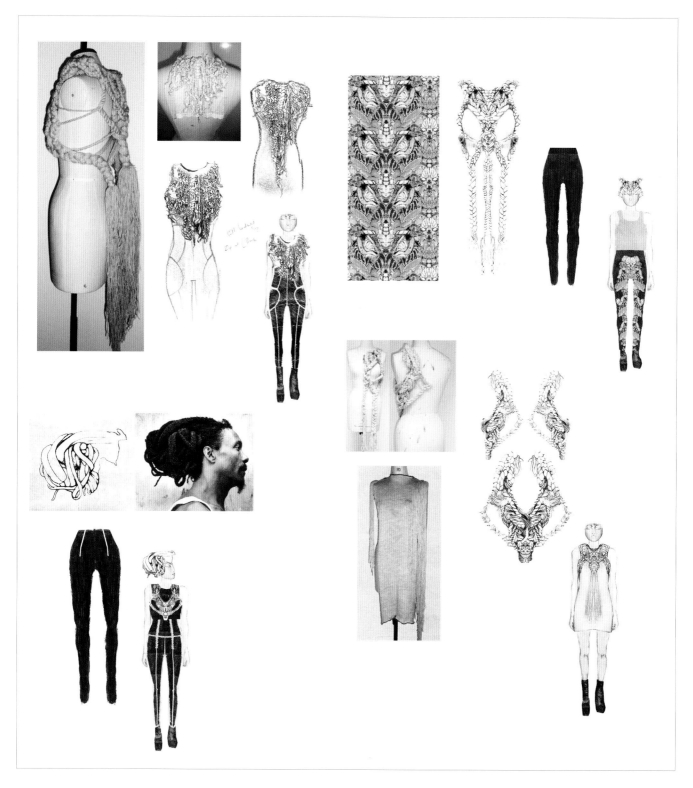

# THE PRODUCTION PROCESS

CREATING AND ANALYSING
A DESIGN

↓

FROM 2D TO 3D
Flat pattern cutting
Modelling on the stand
Combination of methods

↓

GARMENT SPECIFICATION

↓

MEASUREMENTS

↓

PATTERN DRAFTING
Fully fashioned
Cut and sew
Seamless knitting

↓

TOILING GARMENT
Development of sample

↓

KNITTING A TENSION SQUARE
Calculating a tension

↓

PATTERN WRITING

↓

PATTERN CALCULATIONS

↓

YARN REQUIREMENTS

↓

GARMENT PRODUCTION
Knit the garment/garment range

↓

BLOCKING AND STEAMING

↓

GARMENT CONSTRUCTION
AND FINISHING
Overlocking
Linking
Hand sewn

Listed below are the different stages of the knitwear production process; however, the order of sequence can vary from designer to designer and company to company. Some designers plan and create the garment or garment range at the same time as the fabric, while other designers are technique-based, starting with the fabric first and then generating ideas for the silhouette, the garment styling and detailing. Yet others may work with the silhouette and then produce the fabric swatches in alignment with seasonal fashion trends.

The stages of design through to production are lengthy, but the following list will give you an idea of your main considerations:

1. Creating and analysing the design – considering the relationship between fabric development and the silhouette and the body.

2. From 2D to 3D – developing the silhouette from a flat two-dimensional drawing into a three-dimensional structural form through flat pattern cutting, modelling on the stand or a combination of both.

3. Garment specification – a technical drawing of the garment illustrating both the front and back of the design, and listing all garment measurements.

4. Measurements – deciding on the sizing of the garment and the amount of ease to allow.

5. Pattern drafting – producing a pattern to scale, working out the position of the style lines, neckline and armhole shapings, sleeves and design features.

6. Toiling the garment – producing a toile or prototype exploring and challenging the design shape for fit and form, and analysing the final proportions of the garment on a body or mannequin.

7. Tension square – knitting a tension square using the selected yarn, appropriate tension and selected stitch structure. An accurate tension reading is taken identifying the number of rows and stitches per inch or centimetre.

8. Pattern calculations – converting the measurements into stitches and rows using the tension-square reading and then calculating all increases and decreases, and general garment shaping.

9. Pattern writing – recording your written instructions clearly in reference to the specification drawing, or charting out your garment shape. Some knitters prefer to work out their patterns mathematically, writing the pattern out in full with clear pattern instructions, while others tend to graph their design out to scale.

10. Yarn requirements – calculation of yarn required necessary to complete your garment design.

11. Garment production – knitting up body blanks or knitting each garment piece to size.

12. Blocking and steam-pressing the body blanks or garment pieces – pinning each individual piece to a pressing mat, ensuring each is at the correct size when pressed.

13. Garment construction and finishing – blocking the garment and selecting the finishing technique appropriate to the garment styling.

A successful garment is produced with patience, so do not rush through any of the listed stages, but work through them systematically; this will enable you to learn new techniques and work out new solutions to problems. The more time you take to plan out your idea, the more successful the result will be.

Feline silk sculptured dress modelled on the stand by Na'ama Rietti.

# CREATING AND ANALYSING YOUR DESIGN

When starting to design, look at your research (see Chapter 2) and then consider the type of garment and the silhouette desired. A design can be created from a very simple shape – for example, a basic dropped-sleeve sweater. It is easy to change the basic shape of the garment design by lengthening, widening or shaping your pattern. At the same time, consider your use of colour, yarn and texture as discussed in Chapter 3, and other factors, such as stitch technique or innovative processes, as discussed in Chapter 4.

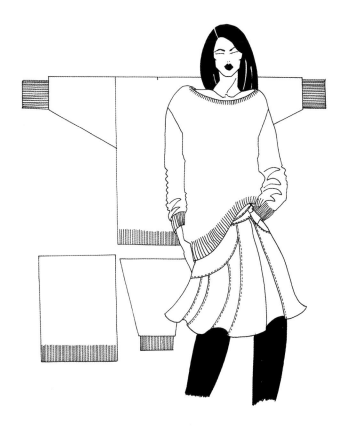

**Below:** Exploring cable, plaiting and partial knitting using hand-knitting techniques, and playing with scale by Marcela Abal and Maria Ines Paysse.

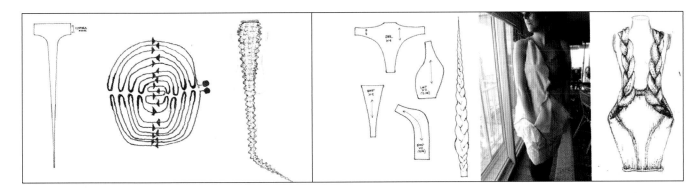

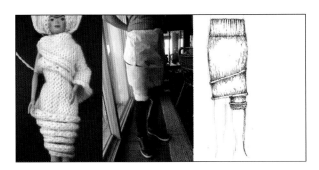

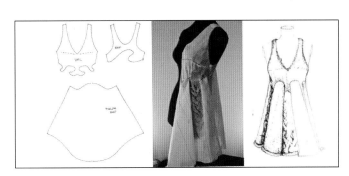

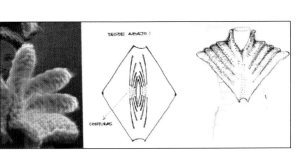

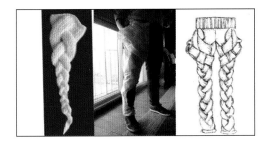

| DESIGN VARIATIONS AND ADJUSTMENTS | |
|---|---|
| Garment type | Coat, jacket, hoodie, poncho, cape, cardigan, ballet wrapped cardigan, twinset, sweater, tank top, vest, camisole, tunic, tabard, gilet, bolero, shrug, dress, skirt, trousers, jumpsuit. (See Style Directory – Chapter 2) |
| Silhouettes | T-shape, A-line, swing, empire, trapeze, cocoon, princess line. |
| Body length | Adjust the body length of the basic block, shortening or lengthening to the silhouette of your design. |
| Width of garment | Widen the basic shape, adding extra width to the body pieces. Consider how the silhouette differs from the basic block, then widen or adjust accordingly.<br><br>Pull the design in at the waistline, using ribbing, tightening the tension or shaping the waistline to give a more fitted look. |
| Shoulder shaping | Consider the shoulder line shaping and design (drop shoulder, square shoulder, saddle shoulder, gathered shoulder detailing or padded shoulder). |
| Neckline styling | Consider openings and finishings, with all adjustments to be made to the basic block to achieve the required neckline shaping (crew, slash, V, square, scooped, boat, drawstring, crossover, sweetheart, keyhole opening, asymmetric, halter, plunge, off-the shoulder, drop-back, polo, funnel, turtle, cowl neck/back or hooded cowl). Think about applying a collar (Peter Pan, split, Bertha, mandarin, grown-on, shirt-style, revere, panelled, draped, shawl or cape).<br><br>Add a hood to the neckline using variations in finishing, such as by shaping the back neckline to form a detachable hood with scarf extension. |
| Armhole shaping | Change the armhole shaping by dropping the shoulder line, setting in the sleeves. Adjust the armhole and sleeve head to achieve the design required (drop, set-in, square armhole, fitted, Raglan, saddle shoulder, kimono, dolman, batwing, flared cape or gathered sleeve head). |
| Sleeve length | Adjust the sleeve length appropriately to the length required, for example full-length, three-quarter length or short cap. |
| Sleeve shape | Consider the sleeve style and shape (straight, fitted, short, flared, cap, puff, extended, flared, Raglan, bishop, gathered sleeve head, bell, batwing, kimono, flared cape or fitted cape). |

| DESIGN VARIATIONS AND ADJUSTMENTS | |
|---|---|
| Cuffs | Consider the cuff length, width, shaping and finish, for example: buttoned, tied, laced, linked, double, turn-back, gathered-in, knitted hem, picot, decorative machine- or hand-knitted trim, drawstring, elasticated, lace, flared, frilled, sewn-down, tabbed, bound, rolled or ruffled cuff, or by using various ribs (1x1, 2x1, 2x2, 3x1, twisted, cable, circular knitted or mock rib – see Chapter 3). |
| Openings and fastenings | Consider the purpose of the openings (functional, practical or decorative) and type of opening (button stand and placket, self-finished, faced plackets, faced finished with buttonholes, shoulder plackets, zip opening – visible, concealed, open-ended or reversible - toggle and tie fastenings, lacings and drawstrings. |
| Pockets | Think about adding pockets to your design, considering the pocket styling, positioning, the size and type of pocket (patch, buttoned-flap patch, box-pleat pouch, side-seam inset, expandable, adjustable or detachable), practicalities and decorative design features. |
| Style lines | Think through the garment style lines: A-line, military style, single- or double-breasted, slim fit, oversized, waterfall or asymmetrical. Consider adding panels or yokes. |
| Hemline | Consider hemline shaping – use shaped, draped, curved, tapered, asymmetrical, unfinished, frayed or distorted hemlines on the garment. Consider adding a peplum, frill, flounce or ribbing to finish. |
| Fastenings | Add fastenings such as buttons, zip fasteners (metal, plastic-moulded, visible, invisible, open-ended, decorative/functional), toggle/frog fastenings, rouleau loops, ties, kilt pin fastenings, buckles, lacings, eyelets, hooks and eyes, or buckles. |
| Decorative edge finishings and trims | Think about edgings and finishings: ruffles, cabling, lace, embroidery, crochet, fabric, elbow patches, faux fur trims, shoulder epaulettes or tassels.<br><br>Incorporate detail such as smocking, ruching, embroidery, beadwork, appliqué, quilting, crochet, reverse and twisted seaming, top stitching, fringing, tassels, leather, suede and woven trims, braids, ribbons, motifs, patchwork, insertions and studding. |
| Construction techniques | Use construction techniques such as fully fashioned, cut and sew, overlocked, linked, decorative and/or innovative seaming, moulding techniques or seamless knitting. |

The above list is by no means exhaustive. With experience, your ideas in pattern drafting and construction will develop, and your designs will become more intricate. Do be careful, however, that the pattern, texture or colourway do not become lost, neglected or spoiled by too many seams, design lines and complicated shaping. Many of the most popular knitwear designers today tend to keep the silhouette simple, relying instead on a play and emphasis on beautiful colourways and intricate stitch structures to create their stunning fabrics.

# ANALYSING YOUR DESIGN FROM 2D TO 3D

After sketching out and exploring all design possibilities, the next stage is to analyse and translate your selected design from a flat, two-dimensional drawing into a three-dimensional wearable garment. Sketch out the front and back views, consider all design possibilities, enlarge detailing and consider the design thoroughly – for example, the type of fastenings, trims, seam finishes and the weight and drape of your fabric.

**Below:** Garment designs with supporting analytical technical drawings by Alexandra Aldridge.

**Right:** When analysing your garment, draw out the front and back of your design as a clear working drawing, as illustrated in this fully fashioned shawl collar sweater design, showing the deep rib at collar, cuffs and hem, which can then be translated into a pattern.

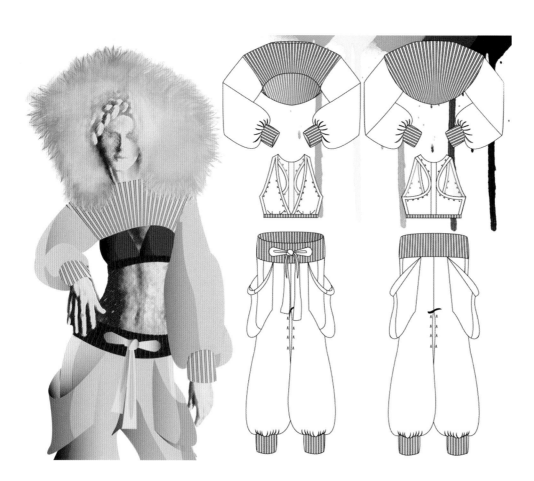

# GARMENT SPECIFICATION

Once you have decided on the final design to be knitted, the next stage is to draw out your design accurately, and preferably to scale, which will help you to appreciate and analyse the proportion of your design. In industry this sketch is known as a specification, schematic or production drawing. This is a clear, analytical drawing using straight lines and clearly labelling the position of pockets, collar types and any other main features. This will help you to work out your design from beginning to end and plan out each stage clearly, giving you complete freedom and a full understanding of each stage of production. Draw out your design in the correct proportions showing ribs and detail. Identify the exact knitted pattern either by illustrating it on your design or by adding notes or attaching a sample(s) to your specification drawing. Industry specification drawings are often produced using computer software for accuracy.

Consider the garment design carefully in relation to the body, think about the type of garment you want, the silhouette, the fit – relaxed, cocoon, trapeze – the neckline, armhole, shoulder and sleeve line and shaping. Make notes as you work, listing information on your drawing, such as length of garment, length of sleeves, references to design detail and so on. You will then be able to refer back to this information easily when drafting and producing your design.

| SAMPLE SIZE SPEC | SIZE RANGE | DEPARTMENT | | |
|---|---|---|---|---|
| Notes: | Date: | Date: | Date: | Date: |
| | Original Sample Specs: | Proto: | 1st Rev: | 2nd Rev: |
| Front body length from hips | | | | |
| Back body length from hips | | | | |
| Chest with 2.5cm below armhole | | | | |
| Across shoulder (seam to seam) | | | | |
| Across front @ 12.7cm from hips | | | | |
| Across back @ 12.7cm from hips | | | | |
| Sleeve length from shoulder | | | | |
| Armhole length straight measure | | | | |
| Sleeve cap height | | | | |
| Sleeve bicep @ 2.5cm from underarm | | | | |
| Sleeve cuff height | | | | |
| Sleeve opening half measure | | | | |
| Shoulder slope | | | | |
| Waist width @ 38cm from hips | | | | |
| Bottom sweep width straight (half measure) | | | | |
| | | | | |
| Neck width seam to seam | | | | |
| Front neck drop | | | | |
| Back neck drop | | | | |
| Neckband width @ CF | | | | |
| | | | | |
| Pocket width | | | | |
| Pocket length | | | | |
| Pocket flap width @ top | | | | |
| Pocket flap length at side | | | | |
| Pocket flap length at centre | | | | |
| Pocket flap width | | | | |
| Top pocket placement from CF | | | | |
| | | | | |
| Front yoke height from hips | | | | |
| Back yoke height from hips | | | | |

**SEASON:**

Date initiated:

NAME:

Descriprition:
**BASIC LONG-SLEEVE KNIT TOP**

Sketch:

Revision comments:

Prepare by:

Approve by:

## CASE STUDY
# ALICE PALMER

Alice Palmer is a knitwear designer who pushes the boundaries of design and production. She is especially interested in pattern, form and shape, creating garments mainly inspired by art and architecture. Unconventional knitting techniques are combined with traditional methods to form garments with a bold and modern look. Her label has a strong, unique aesthetic, coupled with sustainable production methods, which result in no fabric waste.

Alice's Spring/Summer 2012 'Interstellar' collection drew inspiration from David Bowie and glam rock, as well as polyhedra, topology and Op Art. This luxurious collection was created in fine knitted silk and bamboo yarns, resulting in light, delicate textures, and the silhouettes featured manipulated tailored forms with softly structured jackets and draped dresses that combined distorted stripes with laddering.

Since graduating from the Royal College of Art with a master's degree, Alice has held fashion shows in London, Tokyo and New York. In September 2008, while showing her Spring/Summer 2009 collection in New York with NY Profile, she was presented with the Best Womenswear Designer award by sponsors, ASOS.

Alice has been nominated for Young Fashion Designer of the Year at the Scottish Fashion Awards, and in 2010 was selected as one of the three finalists for Fashion Fringe at Covent Garden.

**What made you go into knitwear design?**
I was first introduced to machine knitting while studying for a BA in Knitted Textiles at the Glasgow School of Art. I found the endless possibilities for colour and yarn combinations really addictive, but it was the excitement of making something from scratch that really got me into knitwear design.

**What is the concept behind your label?**
I combine traditional knitting techniques with unconventional methods to form garments, using production methods that are friendly to the environment, involving no fabric waste.

**Can you describe your design process in a few sentences?**
I use a technique which I developed specially while completing my masters at the Royal College of Art (2005–7). Called 'Polyhedra', this is a three-dimensional knitting technique resulting in 'peaks' within the fabric straight from the machine, caused by the positioning of high and low butts, teamed with racking and the use of the tucking cams.

**What types of machine do you use in the production of your work?**
I use Dubied industrial machines for sampling in the studio and then Shima Seiki machines at the factory for production.

**Do you flat pattern cut, model on the stand or use a combination of techniques in the development of your designs?**
Most of the time I drape and develop ideas on the stand, as it is fundamental for me to be able to work around the body, and also important to consider placement directly on the form.

**Left:** Design by Alice Palmer – 'the 'Interstellar' Spring/ Summer 2012 collection, inspired by glam rock.

**Below:** Monochrome pink fitted dress inspired by the glam rock of David Bowie's Ziggy Stardust with Op Art overtones, from the 'Interstellar' collection.

**Who or what have been your biggest inspirations artistically?**

I am mainly inspired by art, architecture, science and films. I have also been influenced by the illusionary and mathematical aesthetics of polyhedra, topology and Op Art – these inspire the form, pattern and the silhouette of the garments.

**What is the key to your success?**

I spent years acquiring my skills and technical knowledge of knitting in order to develop a unique aesthetic, which is very important for a brand in this competitive industry, but the main key to my success has to be perseverance.

**What is your biggest fashion achievement to date?**

My biggest fashion achievement was when I was picked by John Galliano to be a finalist for Fashion Fringe at Covent Garden, in 2010.

**What is your advice to someone who wants to establish their own fashion/knitwear label?**

To make the most of opportunities, be well prepared when opportunities do arise and most importantly – to never give up.

# TAKING MEASUREMENTS

The next stage of the design process is to note down the required measurements of the person for whom you are designing. A measurement sheet is useful for recording them in an organized way, carefully and accurately. It can be filed away for future reference and used for checking sizing and tension, for example.

**Bust/chest measurements** – Measure around the fullest part of the bust. For men and children always measure with the chest fully expanded, making sure that the tape measure is lying horizontal and not twisted at the back. Add ease as required.

**Shoulder width** – Measure across the back, shoulder to shoulder. This measurement is important when designing a garment with set-in sleeves.

**Waist** – Put the tape measure around the waist, letting it fit comfortably around the natural waistline. This measurement is important when designing dresses, skirts, leggings and trousers – either if the garment sits on the waist, or to add ease according to the style.

**Hips** – Measure around the fullest part of the hips, adding ease as required. This measurement is important when designing skirts and trousers. Remember that the wearer should be able to bend and sit in comfort.

**Centre back length** – Measure from the base of the neck at the back down to the length required.

**Welt** – Measure around the body at the position at which you want the welt to sit, adding ease appropriate to the personal fit of the garment.

**Back neck to wrist** – This measurement is very important when designing a T-shape, saddle shoulder, dolman or similar style garment. Have your model stand with their arm extended and slightly bent. Take the measurement from the base of the neck to the wrist or to the point on the arm at which the sleeve should end.

**Shoulder to cuff measure** – Measure from the shoulder point to wrist. This measurement is useful for set-in sleeve styles.

**Underarm** – Always measure around the fullest part of the arm, adding sufficient ease for comfort or garment styling.

**Wrist measurement** – Measure around the wrist bone and also around the knuckles with the hand lying flat, then compare these measurements; you need to allow enough space for the hand to go through the cuff comfortably.

**Skirt length** – Measure from the natural waistline to the required length of the skirt, measuring down the side of the body for accuracy. The measurements required will depend on the design and the type of garment being produced.

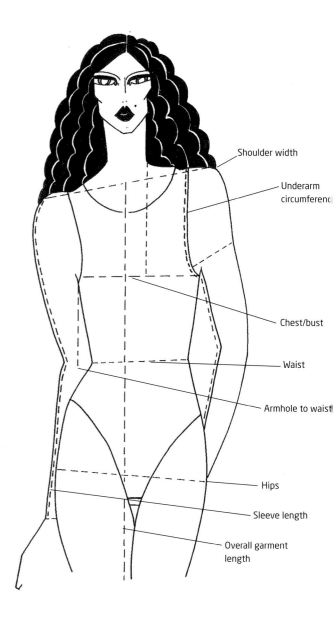

Shoulder width

Underarm circumferenc

Chest/bust

Waist

Armhole to waist

Hips

Sleeve length

Overall garment length

## EASE

**When measuring for a knitted garment, always allow ease. Ease is the extra amount added to a person's measurements to ensure a comfortable and relaxed garment fit, allowing for movement. The exact amount of ease required varies, depending on the style and the shape of the garment. The amount of ease will differ from woven fabrics as knitted fabrics have much more elasticity and stretch.**

**An easy way to determine the amount of ease is to measure a similar-shaped garment that fits in the desired way. In general, for a skin-tight fit add 5cm to a chest or bust measurement, as this gives a minimum allowance for movement, and for a baggy, loose-fitting sweater allow 15–23cm, or even more, depending on the look you want to achieve.**

| MEASUREMENT RECORD SHEET | |
|---|---|
| **MEASUREMENTS FOR:** | **DATE:** |
| (a) Chest/bust | |
| (b) Shoulder width | |
| (c) Armhole depth | |
| (d) Armhole to waist | |
| (e) Garment length total | |
| (f) Waist | |
| g) Hips | |
| (h) Underarm circumference | |
| (i) Width of sleeve at cuff | |
| (j) Sleeve length | |
| (k) Neck width | |
| (l) Skirt length | |

Once you have noted the body measurements and added the required amount of ease for the style, you should then note down the above measurements and add them to your specification drawing.

# GARMENT SPECIFICATION SHEET
## TENSION SWATCH AND GARMENT INFORMATION

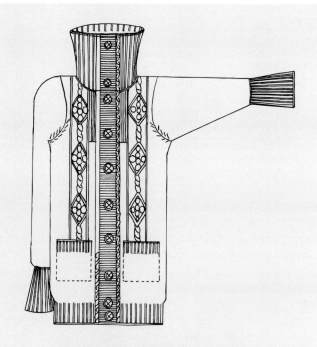

**Garment description:**
Fully fashioned cardigan with set-in sleeves and inset pockets with horizontal opening and ribbed trim. Deep rib collar, flared ribbed cuffs and ribbed hem with contrasting colour trims.

**Design no:** 270

**Date:** Autumn/Winter 2013/2014

**Yarns:** Sublime Cashmere Merino

**Fibre content:** Silk DK, extra fine merino wool, 20% silk and 5% cashmere.

**Tension swatch and ribbing detail:** Decorative double cable with relief laddering (as attached)

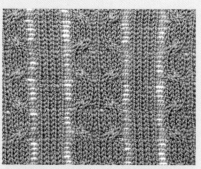

**Tension ribbing:** T4

**Tension main:** T6. Standard

**Stitch structure ribbing:** 2 x 2 rib

**Ribbing tension:**
Sts................cms

**Stitch structure main:** Decorative cable patterning with bobble trim insertion and ladder detailing

**Main tension:**
Sts................cms

**Front knitted band:** Horizontal front knitted ribbed band worked separately

**Trims:** 10 x 4 hole green buttons (No: JR2067)

**Pockets:** 2 x front inset pockets with rib detailing

# PATTERN DRAFTING

Once you are happy with your design, the next step is to draft the pattern. There are two methods of pattern drafting: modelling on the stand and flat pattern cutting – or a combination of the two. Initially pattern drafting may appear very daunting. However, if viewed as simply part of the design process required to develop your garment shape, it can be a satisfying, creative activity.

## MODELLING ON THE STAND

Modelling on the stand is also known as 'draping'. This is the development of a design idea by manipulating and sculpting paper or a similar-weight fabric to your knit, pinning it on a dress stand or mannequin, and thus creating and developing your garment design three-dimensionally; a process that can produce new silhouettes. By manipulating the fabric a design is developed, which then needs to be translated into a flat pattern. As you work it is useful to take photographs of your design from all angles, including the design details, documenting your ideas for future reference.

**Above:** 'Shake it, Spray it, Shake it' collection, inspired by graffiti, urban street culture and '80s female hip-hop artists, designed and modelled on a stand by Alexandra Aldridge.

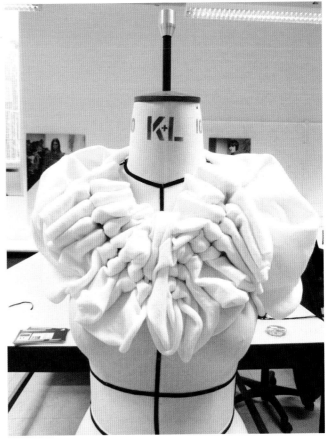

**Right:** Draping, sculpting and moulding fabric on a dress stand or mannequin allows you to experiment three-dimensionally, as illustrated in this neckline detailing by Clare Mountain at Threadbare.

You will need to use a tape measure, scissors, felt-tip pens and steel pins to shape and sculpt your ideas. Use a felt-tip pen to mark the straight grain of the fabric, the neckline, and to identify any strategic points such as the bust point and waistline on your fabric. Once the garment design is completed, the fabric is sewn together carefully to create a toile, and the size, fit, amount of ease, garment proportions and drape are then checked by being modelled on a person of the correct height and proportions. This gives you the opportunity to review the final garment shape and fit.

Once you are satisfied with the results, the toile is then unpicked and the pieces are traced around to create the pattern pieces. It is useful to label your pattern clearly to identify the front, back, side panel, waistband, etc. Modelling on the stand allows the designer total freedom to explore shape, structure and form through sculptural draping, pleating and tucking of fabrics to create interesting design features and explore detailing, which can then be transformed into knit.

Creating and manipulating a design on the mannequin using partial knitting techniques, by Beatrice Korlekie Newman.

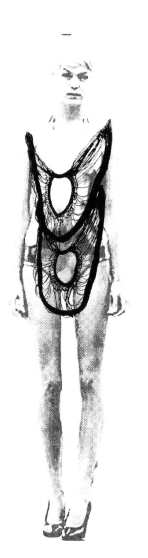
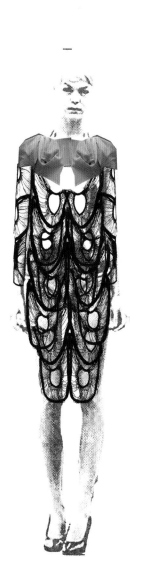
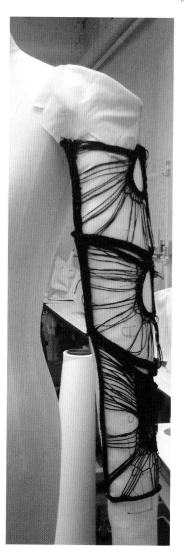

# FLAT PATTERN CUTTING

Flat pattern cutting is the method of creating and using a basic block or pattern shape. Once created, you trace around the block and adapt the shape to your design adding style lines, flare, pleats, gathers or panels to create the garment silhouette. This tends to be a more mathematical approach to developing a design, as each adjustment is calculated and drawn with the aid of a ruler or curve. There is also the need to be able to visualize your design three-dimensionally while working two-dimensionally. The pattern is then made up into a toile, which is a sample garment enabling you to check the fit and adjust accordingly. In industry flat pattern cutting is often done using computer software; however, many designers still work by hand, drawing around a basic block and working directly on it to explore and develop their pattern.

You will already have worked out the basic shape in the form of a schematic drawing, as illustrated on page 184, noting down all the relevant measurements for each section and adding sufficient ease for practical and aesthetic reasons.

**There are several methods of producing your own pattern shape or basic block:**

◆ Following a commercial pattern, using the suggested yarn and stitch pattern, and then adapting the design by adding your own ideas, such as working out a different colour scheme, adding trimmings, edgings and fringing, and choosing a manufacturing method.

◆ Using four rectangles as your basic shape, (two for the front and back, and two for the sleeves) can be a very versatile starting point for creating your own design. This produces a useful introduction to pattern drafting, as no difficult shaping and calculation is required. From this basic shape you can then experiment by adapting and developing your own silhouette.

◆ Using a commercial dressmaker's paper pattern for the basic shape. This can be taken and adjusted to fit your own design. To lengthen a design, add the length in the main body of the garment and below the armhole shaping; adjust the length of a skirt below the hipline in the straight section of the skirt.

◆ Working a full-size basic block, giving you the added advantage of creating your own individual shape and adding your own design lines, yokes and panels, which allows you to see the design in its finished proportions.

◆ Many hand and sewing-machine patterns now have production/schematic drawings illustrating the garment shape and measurements. These can be adapted and developed into a series of workable blocks.

# DRAFTING A BASIC BLOCK

Knitwear patterns are usually much simpler in shape than those created for woven fabrics because a knitted fabric will stretch to fit the three-dimensional shape of the body without the need for darts and complicated shaping. Basic block shapes for knitted garments are, therefore, often quite simple. Draft a basic block using your measurements, including the allowance for ease.

1. It is easier to draft half the block so, taking a large piece of card or paper, a pencil and a ruler or set square, draw a long vertical line down one side marking the centre of your block. Construct a rectangle that is half the chest measurement in width by the length of your garment. Then mark in half the width of the neck, the depth of the neck, the shoulder width and shoulder drop. Calculate the armhole depth, measuring from the shoulder to the underarm point, adding any additional allowances and ease, depending on the style of the garment. The step from the shoulder down to the armhole point is half the sleeve-head measurement.

2. Draft the curve of the front neckline shaping using a set square and French curve, starting approximately halfway down the neck depth. This can be calculated by measuring a similar-shaped garment and finishing about midway on the front neck width. Curve the armhole edge using a set square and a French curve.

3. The finished basic bodice block acts as a template to develop and adapt to produce patterns for your design shapes. Once you have produced your first garment from your own block you will work out particular measurements to suit your requirements and design styles. Through trial and error you will improve your garment shape by steadily working out your design from the beginning, taking each step slowly and analysing your design thoroughly.

As mentioned earlier, always remember that the most successful garments are usually designed using simple shapes, incorporating interesting colour combinations, stitch structures and textures for effect.

A basic block can be used to draft out any garment shape by adapting and developing the length and width, and for creating new and innovative garment shapes.

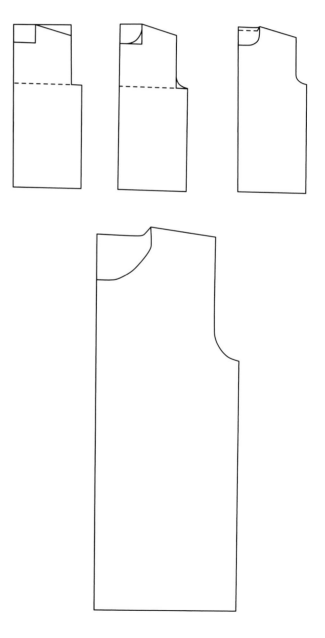

## Necklines and shaping

Consider the finish of the neckline, as this may affect its width and depth. A neckline with a ribbed finish, for example, will have different proportions to a neckline where a draped hood is to be added.

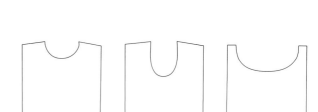

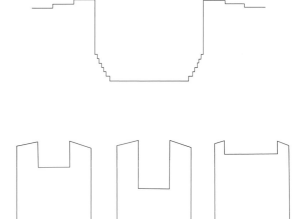

There are many variations in shaping the neckline that can be added to your design. Look at your design and plot the shape out using graph paper, working out the neckline shaping to your tension square calculations.

There is a large variety of neckline styles, as shown in the Style Directory (see pp. 172–73). For a classic round neckline it is usual to allow 16–18cm for the basic neck width for a woman and 21–23cm for a man. The neck depth is approximately half this measurement, although both these sets of measurements will vary, depending on the specific style of the design. If you are unsure about the amount to allow, take measurements from a similar style of garment and apply the measurements to your own work. Alternatively, you can buy measured neckline templates.

Plot the shape of your neckline design onto graph paper using your tension calculations to guide you in your pattern workings. This can be completely square or with the design slightly rounded off, as illustrated, giving a softer appearance.

By carefully planning and drafting your block you will be able to expand easily on the basic classic round-neck styling, working and calculating different neckline shapes. A polo neck, for example, is worked in a similar way to the round neck, though the front neck depth is shallower and the front and back neck width are increased in proportion, giving the same circumference. A cowl neck is drafted much wider – at 26cm, for example – but has a shallower neck depth.

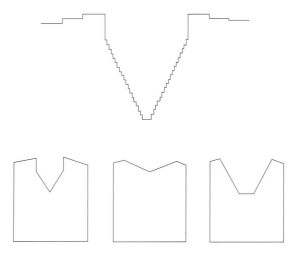

V-neck shaping.

## Drafting a sleeve block

1. Once again, it is easier to draft only half the sleeve, so draw a vertical line down one side of a piece of paper, marking the centre of the sleeve. At the bottom of the line, draw in half the width of the cuff. With a set square mark in the full width of the sleeve as a horizontal line. The horizontal line represents the width of the sleeve at the base of the sleeve head, which is calculated by measuring around the armhole on your main body block. Draw a diagonal line from the top of the vertical line to end of the horizontal line.

2. Draw a curved line for the sleeve head, starting at the top of the vertical line with a convex curve, and then reversing the curve to draw a concave curve down to the horizontal line, which is the underarm point. This should measure the depth of the sleeve head. Draw in the shape of the cuff.

3. Draw a line from the underarm point down to the top of the cuff to create the underarm seam to finish the sleeve block. This can be adapted to your own personal shape.

Once the full-scale design is drawn out, you can then begin to appreciate the proportions of the garment, which will help you decide how deep you want a border pattern to be, the position of a yoke or the width of a front button stand.

The basic block and sleeve block can be drawn around and adapted and developed, adjusting the garment at strategic points, for example by cinching in the waist, forming a yoke or changing the sleeve shape.

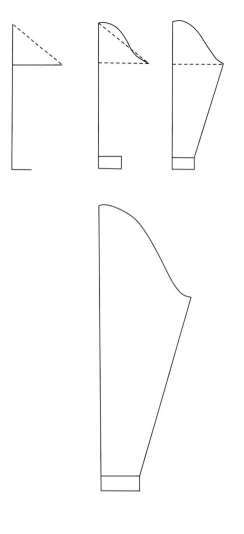

**Top:** Drafting a basic sleeve block.

**Right:** Garment lines for pattern adaption.

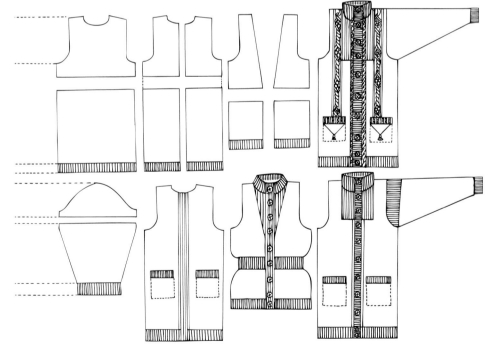

# KNITTING AND CALCULATING TENSION

Knitters often underestimate the need to knit a tension square before knitting the actual garment. Tension (also known as 'gauge') is used to determine how many stitches and rows per inch or centimetre are needed to knit the required shape or garment. Only by carefully checking that the correct tension is being knitted can the designer be sure that the finished product will be produced to the correct size and shape. A tension square will allow you to measure the knit tension and to calculate how many stitches to cast on, how many rows to knit, and where to increase and decrease.

First select the yarn and stitch pattern to be used in your design, and then decide on the appropriate gauge or tension for the swatch to be knitted in. This is a personal judgement, usually based on experience. If you are unsure, however, produce a series of tension squares in various tensions. This will allow you to compare the texture, weight and thickness of the fabrics and select the tension most appropriate to your design, carefully considering the quality and handle of the fabric produced.

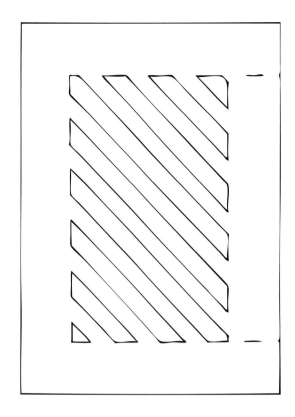

**Top:** Knitting a tension square or tension swatch is important in producing an accurate well-fitted garment.

**Left:** Careful measuring of a tension square is required to calculate the number of stitches and rows needed to produce a garment to the correct size and shape.

IF YOU USE A
COMMERCIALLY BOUGHT
KNITTING PATTERN ALWAYS
CHECK THE TENSION,
MAKING ADJUSTMENTS
WHERE NECESSARY.

## YARN TENSION IN MACHINE KNITTING

In domestic machine knitting, the setting of the break yarn tension disc is important for two reasons:

◆ The spring in the disc controls the flow of the yarn, giving a constantly even tension. This prevents loops forming at the sides of your knitting, which is a common problem for beginners.

◆ The disc also prevents the problem of yarns getting tangled up in the knitting carriage.

Remember to always set the tension disc according to the thickness of the yarn used. The use of the wax disc helps the yarn to feed through the yarn tension unit and carriage, allowing you to knit more smoothly. Waxing the yarns also prevents brittle yarns from breaking and helps highly textured yarns to run into the carriage without getting tangled up in the process.

## YARN TENSION IN HAND KNITTING

The tension will vary depending on the individual knitter, the type of yarn used and the size of needle. It is important, therefore, for the hand knitter to produce samples exploring the tension of the knitting required by testing it out before producing the pattern and garment.

Always knit a sample large enough for you to measure it in several places to get an accurate tension reading; a 20cm square is ideal.

Once the tension square has been knitted, it must be allowed to relax after being stretched across the knitting needles. The longer you leave the tension square before steaming or pressing, etc., the more accurate the tension reading will be. Always leave it to rest after pressing, too, as fabrics will relax again. It is important to treat the tension square exactly as you would the finished garment (pressing, cold blocking and so on).

Place the tension square on a flat surface and mark a 10cm square in the middle using waste yarn. Always measure within this area for an accurate reading, as the edge of your sample swatch may be distorted. Count the number of stitches and rows to the centimetre.

It is also important to check the compatibility of stitch patterns. For example, on a sweater a contrasting yoke design, introducing a secondary pattern to the design, must be complementary to the main body stitch structure and be compatible in tension, weight and appearance. Therefore, if you intend to use two or more stitch patterns in any one garment, take time to get the yarn weights, stitch and fabric structure to work together. A tension sample should be knitted for both the rib and main body.

# PATTERN CALCULATIONS

To work out your pattern, each section of the garment must be calculated exactly. Work out the number of stitches and rows required to knit each garment piece by multiplying the measurements of the garment by your tension-square calculation.

An example calculation:

Tension reading = 25 stitches and 30 rows to 10cm (2.5 stitches and 3 rows to 1cm)

To knit a square of 45cm x 45cm:
45cm x 2.5 stitches = 112.5 (round up or down to a whole figure; therefore 112 stitches)
45cm x 3 rows = 135 rows

Therefore, if you were knitting a square of 45cm x 45cm, you would cast on 112 stitches and knit 135 rows.

To shape by increasing or decreasing, translate all measurements into the number of stitches per centimetre and the number of rows per centimetre and calculate the difference between the starting point of the section to be increased or decreased and the finishing point, subtracting one from the other to find the difference in size.

For an even distribution, the number of stitches should then be divided by two (to allow for increasing or decreasing on both sides of the body or sleeve piece). For example, shaping a sleeve by increasing, if there are 70 stitches to be added (35 stitches on each side) over 140 rows, divide 140 rows by 35 stitches giving the calculation of 4. This means, if you wanted the increase to be distributed evenly, you would increase by 1 stitch each side of the sleeve every fourth row, 35 times, until you had knitted 140 rows.

70 stitches ÷ 2 (sides of the sleeve) = 35 stitches to increase each side of the knitting

140 rows (length of sleeve) ÷ 35 stitches = 4 rows

Therefore increase by 1 stitch each side of the knitting every 4 rows.

If the calculation is not obviously divisible, it can either be rounded up or down to make it exact. Alternatively, the garment shaping can be drafted out on graph paper and the spacing increases or decreases can be distributed to give the best shaping. In other cases you may want more fullness at a particular point in the garment, so the distribution of increasing or decreasing could be calculated at this point.

# PATTERN WRITING

At first pattern writing appears very complicated, but with a little practice it gets much easier. When writing your own patterns it is important to write down your exact method in a notebook or on your schematic drawing (see p.175) so that you can refer back to it later. Things to note include:

◆ A clear description of the garment
◆ A list of all the measurements
◆ The stitch setting on the machine for the main knitted fabric
◆ The stitch setting for ribs or any other stitches used
◆ The yarn details, including colour, type, dye number and manufacture
◆ The tension for main fabric and ribs
◆ The casting on and casting off method.

For a scooped-neck cardigan the instructions would be as follows overleaf.

**FRONT VIEW**        **BACK VIEW**

**Description:** Write details of the garment design, for example:
Ribbed cardigan with waist cable detailing and belted tie, deep cable rib trims at neckline, cuffs and hem, and on patch pockets.

Abbreviations:
T = Tension/gauge
MT = Main tension/gauge
RT = Rib tension/gauge
Sts = Stitches

**Back:** Cast on (X) sts, knit (X) rows in rib at T (X), change to T (X), and continue in main fabric for (X) rows, and then cast off as follows for the armholes, decreasing as calculated on graph.
Shape armholes by casting off (X) stitches at the beginning of the next (X) rows.
Knit (X) rows to the shoulder to begin shoulder shaping.
Shape shoulders: cast off xx stitches at the beginning of the next and the following alternative row.
Cast off the remaining back neck stitches.

**Left front:** Cast on (X) sts, using T (X). Complete as back up to armhole shaping.
Shape armholes by casting off (X) stitches at the beginning of next row, work 1 row and then decrease (X) stitches at armhole edge of next (X) rows, then knit (X) rows to neckline shaping.
Neckline shaping: Work for neckline as follows, cast off (X) sts at the beginning of next row, (X) sts remaining.
Decrease (X) sts at neck edge of next (X) rows, then on following (X) rows. Continue knitting straight for (X) rows.

**Shape shoulders:** Cast off (X) sts at the beginning of next and following alternate rows. Work (X) rows and cast off.

**Right front:** Work as given for left front, reversing all shapings.
Sleeves (both alike): Cast on (X) sts in rib using T (X) and knit (X) rows. Change to T (X) and continue in main fabric, increasing 1st stitch at each end of every (X) row until (X) rows are knitted and (X) sts are on needles. Knit straight for (X) rows and then cast off.

**Neckband:** Stitch one shoulder seam together and pick up (X) stitches round the neckline, knit (X) rows and then cast off.

**Knitted belt:** Cast on (X) rows and knit straight for (X) rows in (X) stitch and then cast off.

**Additional notes:** Include any information and instructions for additional pattern pieces, collars, attaching ribs, inserting zips and adding buttons.

**Making up:** Add notes for making up and construction techniques.

Patterns will vary greatly depending on the technique and methods applied, and much of the information can be abbreviated even more. When starting to write your own knitting patterns look at the layout of commercial knitting patterns and compare them to your own requirements. Companies have their own formats and once you understand the basics they are easy to adapt to your own specifications.

# CALCULATING YARN REQUIREMENTS

The **yarn count** is the weight per unit length of a yarn, and knowing this enables you to calculate how much yarn is required to produce a garment. There are several different systems used internationally to measure this. These include the denier system and the tex system, both of which calculate the unit of weight in grams. There are many websites that provide full details of conversion, comparison charts and in-depth information about each system, which you may find useful references.

Single ply, 2 ply, 3 ply, 4 ply, double knit, chunky or Aran refer to the number of threads (plies) twisted together to form a yarn; ply is usually referred to in hand knitting.

It is difficult to calculate the exact amount of yarn required for any one garment, depending as it does on the size of a garment, and the yarn required for different stitch structures. It is, however, possible to estimate by measuring your tension square and multiplying it by the width and length of the garment pieces required. It is advisable to add an additional 10 per cent allowance to this calculation. Knitting calculators are also a useful aid and can help with estimating the total yarn needed to complete a project.

**Below:** The laundering and care instructions will be clearly identified on the yarn label, along with the manufacturer's trademark and important information listing fibre content, the weight of the yarn and the dye lot number. The dye lot number indicates which batch of dye the yarn came from, as each will vary slightly in shade.

**Bottom:** Skeins of yarn made from wool of Navajo-churro sheep by local Navajo woman, Lorraine Herde. It is important to have a good working knowledge of the characteristics and composition of yarn, the fibre content, the ply and the structure of the finished fabric to knit a successful garment.

# GARMENT PRODUCTION

Once you have completed your design analysis, produced, checked and made any amendments to the toile, and have sampled and calculated your tension square, it is time to start knitting. As discussed, some designers work intuitively on the stand, modelling, shaping and creating their design, while other designers plan out and fully calculate each component of the garment either by hand, electronically or using a computer program.

Knit the garment to your specifications, whether you are knitting fully fashioned and knitting each piece of the garment to shape, increasing and decreasing following your pattern to shape the garment, or whether you are using cut and sew, knitting a length of fabric or a blank and then cutting the garment to shape after knitting and pressing.

## BLOCKING AND PRESSING KNITTING

When blocking and pressing, your aim is to ease each garment piece to the exact size of your pattern. Use a padded mat or a pressing table and steel pins to block and press your work, pinning the knitting neatly at regular intervals, avoiding any distortion of the fabric. Never pin out or press the ribbing of the garment as this will remove the elasticity and also flatten the ribbing. Be very careful not to over-press your tension sample or your garment pieces, but steam them gently and then leave them to relax.

Once the knitting has relaxed, unpin the pieces and make up the garment to the design required.

Preparing for steaming and pressing the garment.

WHEN JOINING KNITWEAR TAKE CARE NOT TO STRETCH THE PIECES BY DISTORTING THE SEAM OR KNITTING.

# GARMENT CONSTRUCTION AND FINISHING

There are several methods of making up knitwear – different types of garment will require a different technique.

## HANDWORKED METHODS

(a) Mattress stitch seaming can be used almost anywhere on a garment, giving a neat and professional finish. It is worked with the right sides of the knitting facing you. Sew sections of the knitting together by picking up the ridges between two edge stitches, alternating from one side of the work to the other, matching up stitch by stitch, continuing to work along the seam edge. This finish works particularly well with stocking stitch, giving an almost invisible join.

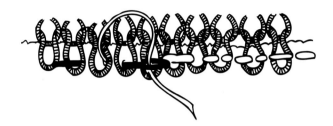

(b) Grafting is a method of joining knitted pieces by hand that produces an invisible seam. This is a technique that can be applied to shoulder seams and for joining ribs to the main body pieces. When working, join the two pieces of knitting together with the right sides facing you and sew them together by picking up an edge stitch on one piece of fabric and then picking up one on the opposite piece, pulling the stitches to the same tension as the knitting.

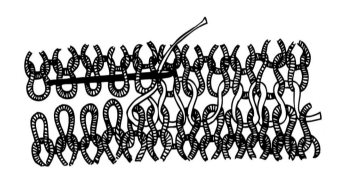

(c) Backstitch seaming is worked by hand and forms a strong, secure seam. It is particularly good for using where a seam needs strengthening, or where there is a lot of strain on the garment, such as at shoulder seams. However, it does tend to be bulky. To work, place the right sides of the knitting together, then work backstitch neatly along the edge, matching all shapings and the pattern design together while working.

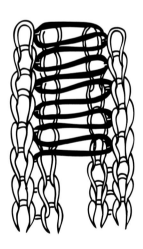

(d) Decorative stitches, such as faggot stitch, can also be used to join two pieces of knitting together, while at the same time creating a feature of the seam via a contrast in stitch structure, colour and/or texture.

Sewing up the garment.

# MACHINE METHODS

## Linking knitting

Linking knitting is the method of joining seams using a chainstitch formation produced on a linking machine. Using the linker with the right sides of the knitting facing you, place the first stitch of the knitting onto the linker points. It is important that the stitches are distributed evenly around the linker. Place the second piece of knitting to be linked onto the linker in the same way but with the wrong side of the fabric facing you, and then work the linker, which will automatically join the two pieces of knitting, forming a neat seam.

## Sewing up knitting

Another method of joining seams is to use a domestic or an industrial sewing machine. This is a quick and easy method of joining seams. Practice is required, however, as it is easy to stretch the knitted fabric and distort the garment shape. Steel pins can be inserted into the knitting to hold the seams together while sewing. Before sewing up your garment always complete a test piece, using a suitable stitch and experimenting with stitch size. A medium zigzag stitch works well on knitwear, as does a straight stitch, but problems can arise if mistakes are made and the work requires unpicking.

## MAKING UP A GARMENT WITH SET-IN OR DROP SLEEVES

When making up a garment with set-in or drop sleeves, join one shoulder seam by using a simple handworked backstitch, grafting the knitting together or linking the seam.

1. Join the shoulder seam
2. Add the neckband, neck finish, collar or trim
3. Join the second shoulder seam
4. Set in the sleeve, easing it carefully to the measured area
5. Join the side seam and the underarm; repeat with the other sleeve.

If transferring hand knitting onto a knitting machine, remember to keep the correct side of the fabric in mind. If you are knitting a Fair Isle design, for example, the purl side of the fabric needs to be facing you. Remember too to alter the machine tension dial to the appropriate tension number, as sampled in your tension square. It is important always to try out a test sample of the hand knitting, transferring it to the machine bed and checking the stitches' compatibility in terms of design, weight and texture. Due to variations in tension and the hand knitting stretching across the machine bed, it is easier to knit the first row manually, allowing for the compatibility in tension.

Left: A range of knitted edgings that can be produced by hand or machine From top sample downwards:

a) Multicoloured picot edge
b) Double picot edge
c) Fluted edge
d) Multicoloured
e) Looped tube trim
f) Decorative eyelet braid

Left: A stable seam can be formed by overlocking the knitting together, which is a method used in industry, and produced by trimming and joining the knitting together in one complete process.

# DECORATING EDGINGS

Decorative edgings offer a versatile finish to any garment. A machine-knitted picot edge, for example, can be inserted into a seam or added as a finishing touch, or stitches can be picked up along an edge and knitted on the front edge of a cardigan or on a sweater base line. Edgings can be produced by machine knitting, hand knitting, crochet or bought ready-made from a manufacturer.

Hand-knitted edges are especially enjoyable to work, particularly if you are both a hand and machine knitting specialist. The two techniques can be easily combined; hand knitting can be simply transferred onto a machine using a transfer tool and machine knitting can be transferred onto hand knitting needles.

**Above:** Instructions for many stunning edgings can be found in any good compendium of knitting stitches and can be worked by hand or machine. From top:
a) Triangular lace edging
b) Victorian lace edging
c) Decorative leaf edging
d) Single frill trim
e) Double frill trim

**Left:** Innovative designs by Sarah Burton, who explores a wide range of techniques, manipulating knit to create original end results.

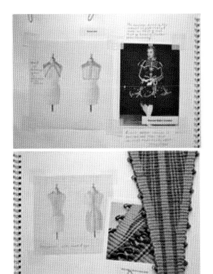

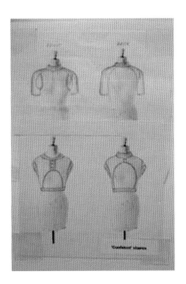

**Above:** Decorative gilt chains inserted into knit by Alexandra Aldridge.

There are many handworked edgings that are simple to work, including multicoloured ribs, striped ribs, textured twisted ribs, cable ribs, and simple lace edgings. Instructions can be found in any compendium of knitting stitches, or alternatively you can experiment and develop your own edgings by varying the yarns and colours that you use.

Many edgings and trims can be completed in a similar way on the knitting machine. All the following edgings are simple to knit and can be produced on a single-bed machine: mock rib, plain hem, picot hem, fluted or scalloped hem, lace edgings, ribs and border designs. The details of these can be found in most knitting-machine manuals, and they all provide ways of finishing a knitted garment, adding further interest with stitch structure, colour and texture. Many knitters avoid trying out lace patterns and decorative trims, thinking that they are too complicated to produce, yet many are actually quite simple to knit and provide an easy way to create contrast in your garment.

Through trial and error you will be able to design your own. Several of the edgings illustrated in this section are created by combining techniques. Some of them, for example, combine simple shaped knitted edging with crochet or bead embroidery to enhance the design and add texture and colour to the trim.

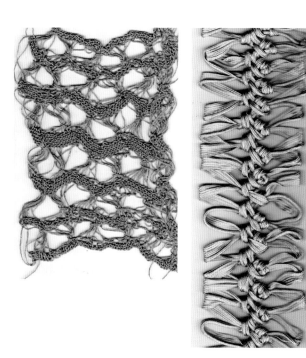

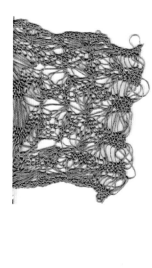

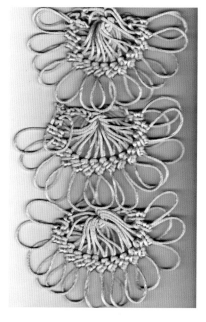

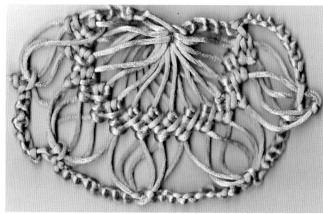

**Above, from left to right:** Decorative macramé and crochet trims by Beatrice Korlekie Newman, which are versatile and can be added to a knitted fabric:

a) Ladder knit and tuck technique
b) Hairpin lace strip
c) Short-row shell stitch
d) Hairpin lace shell technique

**Right:** Decorative hairpin lace trim by Beatrice Korlekie Newman.

## Rib edgings

Ribbing is produced by using both knit and purl stitches in a variety of combinations to form different and interesting rib structures. You can use ribbing to good effect on sleeves, cuffs and body edgings, creating neat, elasticated edgings, which can be adjusted to various sizings by drawing in the knitting.

Hand-knitted ribs work particularly well and provide a good alternative to mock ribs if you do not possess a machine ribber. They can be applied to machine-knitted garments, but often they offer little or no elasticity, making it difficult to stretch across the machine needles used to knit the main body garment. A simple solution to this problem is to hand-knit the edging and then to continue knitting several rows of the machine-knitted design by hand, changing the knitting needles to the size required to keep the hand knitting consistent with the main machine-knitted pieces. If there are fewer stitches in the rib than in the main garment piece, complete an increase row prior to transferring the piece onto the knitting machine bed.

Interesting hand-knitted ribs include: 1 x 1 twisted rib, farrow rib and tweed stitch rib.

**Right:** Ridged 1 x 1 rib attached to sideways knit, adding dimension to fabric by Alexandra Aldridge.

**Below:** Directional knitting and seam finish by Alexandra Aldridge.

## Machine-knitted edgings

There are many different decorative machine-knitted edgings that can be applied to your knitting, such as picot, multicoloured or double picot, plaited edgings attached to borders, fluted trims and rouleau loop trims.

**Above:** 2 x 2 rib structure.

**Right:** 2 x 2 ridged rib design by Alexandra Aldridge .

**Bottom right:** Gilt and silver chains trim added to ribbed fabric by Alexandra Aldridge.

# GLOSSARY

**A**

**Aran** – highly textured style of knitting that takes its name from the Aran Islands in Scotland and is characterized by the complex cables, bobbles, and crossed and embellished stitch patterns of traditional fishermen's sweaters.

**B**

**block** – a body shape pattern used in flat-pattern cutting and adapted and refined to create a pattern of the garment design.

**blocking** – the pinning out of knitting or individual garment pieces to the correct size on a pressing mat ready for steaming.

**body blank** – a knitted rectangle of fabric with a rib or hem that is the correct length and width of the garment shape used in cut-and-sew knit production.

**C**

**colour forecasting** – the prediction and promotion of colours for forthcoming seasonal trends.

**colour matching** – matching a colour identically or working one colour with another complementary colour to match a colour scheme.

**colourways** – different colour combinations in a design.

**cut and sew** – method of garment creation where the garment components are cut from fabric blanks and then the garment pieces are overlocked and sewn together. It contrasts with fully fashioned.

**D**

**denier** – the density of yarn fibres.

**draping** – the process of moulding and sculpting the fabric three-dimensionally onto a mannequin to realize a design. Also known as working or modelling on the stand.

**E**

**ease** – in pattern cutting, an additional measurement calculated between the garment and the actual measurements of the body to allow for the movement and comfort of the wearer.

**F**

**Fair Isle** – traditional technique originating from Fair Isle in the Shetlands of knitting two or more colours in one row of knitting, with the unused colours or yarn floats stranded across the back of the work. This produces all-over multicoloured pattern repeats.

**filament fibres** – a thinly spun thread or fibre that is continuous and can therefore be any length needed.

**flat pattern cutting** – the method of using a basic block or pattern shape to trace around and adapt the shape to the garment design by adding style lines, flare, pleats, gathers or panels to create a garment.

**fully fashioned** – method of creating knitwear where each garment piece is knitted exactly to the shape required by increasing and decreasing the number of stitches, and shaping to the calculated measurements of the garment design. It contrasts with cut and sew.

**G**

**gauge (machine)** – in knitting machine specification, the number of needles in 2.5cm of the knitting machine needle bed.

**graffiti knitting** see knit bombing.

**grafting** – method of hand-sewing knitting together which produces an invisible seam.

**H**

**hand flats** – hand-operated, industrial knitting machines often used by independent designers and small businesses due to the hand operation and the versatility of the machines in the stitch capabilities.

**I**

**intarsia** – also known as colour blocking, knitting two or more blocks of colour in a row. It is an ideal technique for knitting large areas such as picture knitting, or knitting geometric or abstract patterns, lettering and large bold design work.

**J**

**jacquard** – multicoloured and patterned knitting produced on a doubled-bed knitting machine, which gives a similar effect in appearance to Fair Isle knitting but without any floats.

**K**

**knit bombing** – also known as knit graffiti, graffiti knitting and guerrilla knitting, a global trend of knitted street art, customizing the environment from personalizing lampposts to railings and public statues.

**knop** – fancy man-made yarn that is textured with small loops at regular or irregular intervals along its length.

**L**

**linking knitting** – the method of joining two pieces of knitting together to form a neat seam, using a chain stitch formation produced on a linking machine, which can be hand-operated or automatic.

**M**

**mercerization** – a treatment for cellulosic fabrics and yarns such as cotton or hemp, which strengthens the fibre and give it a lustrous appearance.

**modelling on the stand** – the development and exploration of a design idea by manipulating and sculpting paper or fabric of a similar weight to your knit onto a dress stand or mannequin – also known as draping.

**moodboard** – an assemblage of inspirational and visually stimulating images and ideas, colour swatches, yarns and textures focused around a selected theme and presented in an interesting and informative way. Also known as a concept or design inspiration board.

**O**

**overlocking** – the method of using an overlock sewing machine, which easily and quickly cuts and automatically trims to sew over the edge of one or two pieces of cloth used for edging, hemming or finishing knit seams.

**P**

**partial knitting** – when part of a row is knitted and then the work is turned before reaching the end of the row, it adds curve and shape to the knitted structure. Also known as short-row knitting.

**pin tucks** – knitting that has been lifted and pinched together to form a small ridge.

**ply** – the number of single fibres or strands twisted or spun together to form the thickness and weight of the yarn.

**primary research** – research undertaken first-hand from original sources or initial data such as observation, questionnaires, direct drawing, photography, museum and gallery visits, which forms part of the initial design process.

**production drawing** – an accurate representation of the design or garment showing both front and back views, and design detailing. See also specification drawing.

**R**

**range building** – the collation of a group of fabrics, yarns or garments that complement each other to create a collection that works cohesively together in concept and balance.

**rouleau knitting** see tube knitting.

**ruched knitting** – a method of manipulating knitting by lifting the stitches from a previous row; the stitches can then be worked evenly or randomly, creating a gathered, three-dimensional effect.

**S**

**schematic drawing** – a technical line drawing showing both front and back views of the garment design, indicating all design features, style lines and detailing, and usually including all garment measurements.

**seamless knitting** – the production of whole garments with 3D shaping, involving little or no cutting and sewing after production, saving time, labour and yarn costs. Used particularly in the underwear, sports- and activewear, and knitwear markets due to the smooth shaping, flattering fit and the comfort factor of no seam.

**secondary research** – information found in books, journals, magazines and on the internet, which investigates and supports primary research.

**shibori** – a Japanese term for the technique of binding, stitching, folding and twisting fabrics to create a pattern when the fabric is dyed.

**short-row knitting** see partial knitting.

**silhouette** – the outline shape of a garment such as trapeze, hour-glass, bell, box shape.

**slub** – an unevenly spun yarn forms slubs, which are thicker than the overall yarn and have little or no twist.

**space-dyed yarn** – yarn that has been dyed in sections in a variety of different colours, giving a multicoloured effect in one strand of yarn.

**specification drawing** – a clear, analytical drawing identifying seam lines and garment detail, including measurements.

**staple fibre** – many yarns are constructed of fibre lengths known as staple fibres, which are usually from a natural source; they can be twisted to form a yarn.

**style line** – a line in a garment that gives shape and contour.

**T**

**technical flats** – a diagrammatic drawing of the garment that illustrates both the front and back of the design and design detailing.

**techno yarn** – innovative and revolutionary yarns.

**tension** – the calculation of how many stitches and rows per centimetre required to knit a given shape or garment. Also known as gauge.

**tension square** – a sample of knitwear produced to take an accurate tension reading to determine the number of rows and stitches per 2.5cm. This is then used to calculate how many stitches to cast on, how many rows to knit, and where to increase and decrease in a garment or knit design.

**toile** – a prototype or sample garment usually made in cotton calico or cotton jersey, exploring and challenging the design shape for fit and form; it can be used to analyse the final proportions of the garment on a body or mannequin.

**trend books** – published by prediction companies and providing updates on new developments within the fashion and knit industry, these promote new themes and colour stories resulting from the introduction of new fibres, textiles, yarns, fabrics and trims.

**trend forecasting** – the business of researching and predicting international seasonal trends up to 18–24 months in advance of the marketplace. It is used in a variety of industries, including fashion, textiles, interiors, cosmetics and the production industries, providing guidance on thematic stories, directional colour palettes, styling, detailing, fabrics, prints, yarns, trimming directions and graphic design ideas.

**tube knitting** – long, narrow tubes of knitted fabric that can be worked by hand or machine, also known as French or rouleau knitting.

**tuck stitch** – a stitch held in place on a needle without being knitted, the yarn then collects on the needle, creating a 'tuck' and adding dimension to the fabric.

**U**

**upcycling** – the process of finding a new purpose for waste and useless items and transforming them into new products of better quality and value.

**W**

**wale** – a line of loops running lengthways, corresponding to the warp of the knitted fabric.

**warp knitting** – the loops of yarn zigzagging and linking in a vertical direction, creating a stable fabric that cannot be unravelled.

**weft knitting** – a continuous looped structure of interlocking stitches or courses extending horizontally that can be knitted with one continuous length of yarn.

**welt** – a knitted edge, sewn in or onto a knitted garment.

**Y**

**yarn count** – a numerical system that defines the thickness or fineness of the yarn and denotes the correlation between length and weight of the yarn.

# RESOURCES

**Contacts**
The following resources and contacts may be useful to you, providing details of organizations, museums, galleries, trade events, yarn and equipment suppliers, internet resources and trend forecasting services:

## Organizations and Associations – UK

**British Fashion Council (BFC)**
Somerset House, South Wing, Strand,
London WC2R 1LA
Tel: +44 (0) 20 7759 1999
Email: info@britishfashioncouncil.com
www.britishfashioncouncil.com

**British Knitting and Clothing Export Council**
UK Fashion Exports
5 Portland Place, London W1B 1PW
Tel: +44 (0) 20 7636 7788
Email: icontact@5portlandplace.org.uk
www.5portlandplace.org.uk

**The British Wool Marketing Board**
Wool House, Sidings Close, Canal Road, Bradford,
West Yorkshire BD2 1AZ
Tel: +44 (0) 1274 688666
Email: mail@britishwool.org.uk
www.britishwool.org.uk

**CAPITB Trust**
RTITB. Access House, Halesfield 17, Telford,
Shropshire TF7 4PW
Tel: +44 (0) 1952 588533
capitbgrants.com

**The Chartered Society of Designers (CSD)**
1 Cedar Court, Royal Oak Yard, Bermondsey Street,
London SE1 3GA
Tel: +44 (0) 20 7357 8088
Email: info@csd.org.uk
www.csd.org.uk

**Crafts Council**
44a Pentonville Road, London N1 9BY
Tel: +44 (0) 20 7806 2500
Email: makerdev@craftscouncil.org.uk
www.craftscouncil.org.uk

**Department for Business, Innovation and Skills (BIS)**
Main Office – 1 Victoria Street, London SW1H 0ET
Tel: +44 (0) 20 7215 5000 or + 44 (0) 20 7215 6740
www.bis.gov.uk

**Design Council**
34 Bow Street, London WC2E 7DL
Tel: +44 (0) 20 7420 5200
Email: info@designcouncil.org.uk
www.designcouncil.org.uk

**Designer Forum**
Designer Forum Studio,
See Emtex, below.

**Design Trust**
12 Reservoir Road, London N14 4BL
www.thedesigntrust.co.uk

**East Midlands Textiles Association (EMTEX) Ltd**
69– 73 Lower Parliament Street,
Nottingham NG1 3BB
Tel: + 44 (0) 115 9115339
Email: enquiries@emtex.org.uk
www.emtex.org.uk

**Fashion Awareness Direct (FAD)**
10a Wellesley Terrace, London N1 7NA
Tel/Fax: + 44 (0) 20 7490 3946
Email: info@fad.org.uk
www.fad.org.uk

**The Framework Knitters Company**
Corah House, The Cottage Homes
Stoughton Road, Oadby,
Leicestershire LE2 4EX
Tel: + 44 (0) 116 271 2171
Email: FWKOadby@aol.com
www.frameworkknitters.co.uk

**The Guild of Machine Knitters**
Email: membership@guild-mach-knit.org.uk
www.guild-mach-knit.org.uk

**Knitting and Crochet Guild**
Unit 4, Lee Mills, St Georges Road, Scholes,
Holmfirth HD9 1RJ
Email: secretary@kcguild.org.uk
www.kcguild.org.uk

**Shell LiveWIRE**
Design Works, William Street, Felling,
Gateshead NE10 0JP
Tel: + 44 (0) 191 423 6229
Email: enquiries@shell-livewire.org
www.shell-livewire.org

**Society of Dyers and Colourists**
Perkin House, 82 Grattan Road, Bradford,
West Yorkshire BD1 2LU
Tel: + 44 (0) 1274 725138
Email: info@sdc.org.uk
www.sdc.org.uk

**The Textile Institute**
1st Floor, St. James's Buildings, Oxford Street,
Manchester M1 6FQ
Tel: + 44 (0) 161 237 1188.
Email: tiihq@textileinst.org.uk
www.textileinstitute.org

**The Textile Society**
Tel: + 44 (0) 20 7923 0031
Email: membership@textilesociety.org.uk
www.textilesociety.org.uk

**The UK Hand Knitting Association**
www.ukhandknitting.com

**The Worshipful Company of Framework Knitters**
**The Framework Knitters Company**
Corah House, The Cottage Homes, Stoughton Road,
Oadby, Leicestershire LE2 4EX
Tel: + 44 (0) 116 271 2171
Email: FWKOadby@aol.com
www.frameworkknitters.co.uk

**UK Fashion Exports (UKFE) and UK Fashion and Textile Association (UKFT)**
3 Queen Square, London WC1N 3AR
Tel: + 44 (0) 20 7843 9460
Email: info@ukft.org
www.ukft.org

**Organizations and Associations – Mainland Europe**

**European Textile Network (ETN)**
P.O. Box 5944, 30059 Hanover, Germany
Tel: + 49 (511) 817006
Email: ETN@ETN-net.org
www.ETN-net.org

**Handknitting Association of Iceland**
Skólavörðustígur 19, 101 Reykjavík, Iceland
Tel: + 354 552 1890
Email: handknit@handknit.is
www.handknit.is

**International Wool Textile Organisation (IWTO)**
Rue de l'Industrie 4, 1000 Brussels, Belguim
Tel: + 32 2 505 40 10
Email: info@iwto.org
www.iwto.org

**Spanish Association of Knitwear Manufacturers**
Av. Diagonal, 474-08006 Barcelona, Spain
Tel: + 34 934 151 228
www.knitting.org

**Texere**
Buchenstrasse 20, 52076 Aachen, Germany
Email: pchristy@talktalk.net
www.texere.u-net.dk

**Organizations and Associations – North America**

**American Wool Council**
www.sheepusa.org

**The Color Association of the United States**
33 Whitehall Street, Suite M3, New York,
New York 10004, USA
Tel: + 1 212 347 7774
Email: info@colorassociation.com
www.colorassociation.com

**Council of Fashion Designers of America**
1412 Broadway, Suite 2006
New York, NY 10018, USA
Tel: + 1 212 302 1821
www.cfda.com

**Craft Yarn Council**
469 Hospital Drive, Suite E, Gastonia,
North Carolina 28054, USA
Tel: + 1 704-824-7838,
www.craftyarncouncil.com

**International Textile and Apparel Association**
PO Box 70687, Knoxville,
Tennessee 37938-0687, USA
Tel: + 1 865-992-1535
Email: info@itaaonline.org
www.itaaonline.org

**The Knitting Guild Association (TKGA)**
1100-H Brandywine Boulelvard, Zanesville,
Ohio 43701-7303, USA
Email: TKGA@TKGA.com
www.tkga.com

**Pantone Colour Institute**
590 Commerce Boulevard,
Carlstadt, NJ 07072-3098, USA
www.pantone.com

**Surface Design Association**
P.O. Box 360, Sebastopol, California 95473-0360, USA
Email: info@surfacedesign.org
www.textilesociety.org

**Organizations and Associations – Australia**

**Australian Fashion Council**
Unit 16, 23–25 Gipps Street,
Collingwood, Victoria 3066, Australia
Tel: + 61 (0) 38680 9400

Email: info@australianfashioncouncil.com
www.australianfashioncouncil.com

**Council of Textile and Fashion Industries Australia Ltd (TFIA)**
Level 2, 20 Queens Road, Melbourne,
Victoria 3004, Australia
Tel: + 61 (0) 38317 6666
Email: info@tfia.com.au
www.tfioa.com.au

**The Woolmark Company**
Level 30, HSBC Centre, 580 George St,
Sydney, New South Wales 2000,
GPO Box 4177, Sydney, New South
Wales, Australia
Tel: + 61 (0) 28295 3100
Email: feedback@wool.com
www.woolmark.com

**Organizations and Associations – Asia**

**China Knitting Industrial Association**
12 East Chang An Street 100742, Beijing, China
Tel: + 86-10—85229417
Email: ckia@163.com
www.cnknit.org

**Fashion Design Council of India**
4th Floor, JMD Regent Plaza,
Mehrauli Gurgaon Road, Gurgaon,
Haryana 122001, India
Tel: + 91 124 4062881/4062882/4062883
Email: contact@fdci.org
www.fdci.org

**Hong Kong Fashion Designers Association**
Room 216A, 2/F, InnoCentre,
72 Tat Chee Avenue, Kowloon Tong,
Kowloon, Hong Kong
Email: mail@hkfda.org
www.hkfda.org

**Textile Council of Hong Kong**
Room 401–403, 4/F, Cheung Lee
Commercial Building,
25 Kimberley Road, 4/F, Tsimshatsui,
Kowloon, Hong Kong
Tel: + 852 2305 2893
Email: sec@textilecouncil.com
www.textilecouncil.com

**Trade Events – UK**

**Knitting and Stitches Show (London, Harrogate, Ireland)**
Creative Exhibitions Ltd. Exhibition House
8 Greenwich Quay, London SE8 3EY
Tel: + 44 (0) 20 8692 2299
Email: mail@twistedthread.com
www.twistedthread.com

**London Fashion Week**
British Fashion Council, Somerset House,
South Wing, Strand, London WC2R 1LA
Tel: + 44 (0) 20 7759 1999
www.londonfashionweek.co.uk

**London Edge and London Central**
Londonedge Ltd. Hazel Drive,

Leicester LE3 2JE, UK
Tel: +44 (0) 116 289 8249
Email: info@londonedge.com
www.londonedge.com

New Designers
Tel: +44 (0) 20 7288 6738
Email: nd@upperstreetevents.co.uk
www.newdesigners.com

**Trade Events – Mainland Europe**

Expofil
20, Boulevard Eugène Deruelle
69432 Lyon, Cedex 3, France
Tel: +33 (0) 4 72 60 65 00
Email: info@premiervision.fr
www.expofil.com

Interstoff
texpertise.messefrankfurt.com

Pitti Immagine Filati Yarn Fair – Florence, Italy
www.pittimmagine.com

Première Vision
Head Office: 20 Boulevard Eugène Deruelle,
69432 Lyon, Cedex 3, France
Tel: +33 (0) 4 72 60 65 00
Email: info@premierevision.fr
www.premierevision.com

Texworld, Paris
Messe Frankfurt France,
1 Avenue de Flandres, 75019 Paris, France
Tel: +33 155 268 989
www.texworld@france.messefrankfurt.com

**Trade Events – North America**

Fashion Week Canada
Email: info@fdcc.ca
www.lorealfashionweek.ca

The International Fashion Fabric Exhibition,
New York
Magic International, 2nd Floor,
6200 Canoga Avenue,
Woodland Hills, CA 91367, USA
Email: cs@MAGIConline.com
www.fabricshow.com

New York Fashion Week
The Waldorf Astoria, 301 Park Avenue,
New York, USA
Tel: +1 212 202 4604
Email: info@ucsafashionshows.com
www.couturefashionweek.com

SPINEXPO, New York
Organizers: Well Link Consultants Ltd
Shui On Centre 2/F, 66-8 Harbour Road
Wanchai, Hong Kong
Tel: +852 2824 8581
Email: info@spinexpo.com
www.spinexpo.com/new-york

Texworld, USA
Messe Frankfurt, Inc.
1600 Parkwood Circle, Suite 615

Atlanta, GA 30339
Tel: +1 770.984.8016 ext.401
Email: twusainfo@usa.messefrankfurt.com
www.TexworldUSA.com

**Trade Events – Asia**

China International Knitting Trade Fair
Unit 1812, 18/F., Wayson Commercial Building,
28 Connaught Road West, Hong Kong
Tel: 852-2-8581916
www.chinaknitting.com.

SPINEXPO, Shanghai
Well Link Consultants Ltd
Shui On Centre 2/F
66-8 Harbour Road, Wanchai, Hong Kong
Tel: +852 2824 8581
Email: info@spinexpo.com
www.spinexpo.com/shanghai

Yarn Expo – China
Messe Frankfurt (HK) Ltd.
3506 China Resources Building
26 Harbour Road, Wanchai, Hong Kong
Tel: +852 2802 7728
Email: info@hongkong.messefrankfurt.com
www.messefrankfurt.com.hk

**Museums and Galleries – UK**

Costume and Textile Study Centre
Carrow House, 301 King Street, Norwich NR1 2TS
Tel: +44 (0)1603 223870
Email: museums@norfolk.gov.uk
www.museums.norfolk.gov.uk

Fashion Museum
Assembly Rooms, Bennett Street, Bath BA1 2QH
Tel: +44 (0) 1225 477789
Email: fashion_bookings@bathnes.gov.uk
www.museumofcostume.co.uk

Knitting History Forum
www.knittinghistory.org

Knitting Together
Leicester City Museums Service, 12th Floor,
A Block New Walk Centre, Welford Place,
Leicester LE1 6ZG
Tel: +44 (0) 116 2527322
www.knittingtogether.org.uk

Ruddington Framework Knitters' Museum
Chapel Street, Ruddington, Nottingham NG11 6HE
Tel: +44 (0) 1159 846 914
www.rfkm.org

Scottish Knit Research Centre (SKRC)
Heriot-Watt University
Scottish Borders Campus, Galashiels, TD1 3HF
Email: enquiries@hw.ac.uk
www.tex.hw.ac.uk

Shetland Museum and Archives
Hay's Dock, Lerwick,
Shetland ZE1 0WP
Tel: +44 1595 695057
www.shetland-museum.org.uk

Victoria and Albert Museum
(Knitting in the Archive of Art and Design)
Blythe House, 23 Blythe Road,
London W14 0QX
Tel: +44 (0) 20 7603 1514
www.vam.ac.uk/content/articles/k/knitting-in
the-archive-of-art-and-design

Winchester School of Art Library
(Knitting Reference Library and
Knitting Collection)
University of Southampton, Park Avenue,
Winchester, SO23 8DL
Tel: +44 (0) 23 8059 8531
Email: wsaenqs@soton.ac.uk
www.southampton.ac.uk/intheloop

**Museums and Galleries – Mainland Europe**

The Danish National Research Foundation's
Centre for Textile Research
The SAXO Institute, University of Copenhagen,
Njalsgade 76, DK-2300 Copenhagen S
Email: CTR@hum.ku.dk
ctr.hum.ku.dk

ModeMuseum Provincie Antwerpen – MoMu
Nationalestraat 28, 2000 Antwerp, Belgium
Email: info@momu.be
www.momu.be

Textile Museum
Audax Textielmuseum Tilburg
Goirkestraat 96, 5046 GN Tilburg, the Netherlands
Email: info@textielmuseum.nl
www.textielmuseum

**Museums and Galleries – North America**

The Costume Institute
The Metropolitan Museum of Art
1000 Fifth Avenue, New York,
New York 10028-0198
Tel: +1 212-535-7710
www.metmuseum.org

The Textile Museum of Canada
55 Centre Avenue,
Toronto, Ontario
M5G 2H5
Tel: +1 416 599-5321
Email: info@textilemuseum.ca
www.textilemuseum.ca

**Museums and Galleries – Australia**

Powerhouse Museum
PO Box K346, Haymarket,
New South Wales 1238, Australia
www.powerhousemuseum.com

**Internet Resources/Useful Websites:**

Yarn and equipment suppliers, knitting blogs and links, news and online magazines:

**Art Yarn**
www.artyarn.org
Online shop selling good selection of yarns, fibres, needles and accessories.

**Craft Yarn Council**
www.craftyarncouncil.com
'The yarn industry's one-stop resource'.

**Culture24**
www.culture24.org.uk
'News, exhibition reviews, links, event listings and education resources from thousands of UK museums, galleries, heritage sites, archives and libraries'.

**Europe Knitting**
www.europeknitting.blogspot.co.uk
Inspirational knitting blog.

**Folksy**
www.folksy.com
British craft site with fibres, yarn and knitting supplies.

**I Knit London**
www.iknit.org.uk
'A sanctuary for knitters', with online shop, selling yarns, equipment and haberdashery: blog, news and details of events.

**Knitting Institute**
www.knittinginstitute.co.uk
Informative website providing yarn reviews, detail techniques, free knitting patterns, forum, gallery and useful links.

**Knittsings**
www.knittsings.com
Excellent source of information and links for machine and hand-knitters.

**Knitting Together**
www.knittingtogether.org.uk
The heritage of the East Midlands knitting industry.

**Knitty**
www.knitty.com
Free knitting magazine on the web published quarterly.

**Knitting History Forum**
www.knittinghistory.co.uk
'Aims to encourage and develop the international, multi-period study of knitting successfully inspired by the late Montse Stanley'. News, events and resources listed.

**The Knitting Industry**
www.knittingindustry.com
Online news and technical resource for the global knitting industry, written and published by knitting industry professionals.

**Knitters' Review**
www.knittersreview.com

A free weekly online knitting magazine dedicated to yarns, tools, patterns and books.

**Pluckyfluff Studio**
www.pluckyfluff.com
Stunning handspun, highly textured yarns.

**Prick your Finger**
www.prickyourfinger.com
A textile art collective, online yarn shop and resource space/gallery.

**Ravelry**
www.ravelry.com
A community site with a good database listing yarns, for knitters and crocheters, spinners and weavers.

**Rowan Yarns**
www.knitrowan.com
Database of current knit designs, yarns, free patterns, newsletter and members-only forum.

**Textile & Apparel WWW Database**
www.tex.in
A comprehensive database offering an excellent resource, and providing information about developments and new technologies in the fibre, yarn and textile industry.

**TextileArts.net**
www.textilearts.net
Web and community resource designed for artists, students, tutors, researchers and businesses involved in art textiles.

**Texere Yarns Ltd**
www.texere-yarns.co.uk
An excellent selection of yarns, special offers, books and patterns.

**Twisted Thread**
www.twistedthread.com
Specialize in organizing creative exhibitions for the public, including the Knitting and Stitching Shows.

**Vogue Knitting**
www.vogueknitting.com
Previews the latest issue of *Vogue Knitting*, yarn finder, charts and patterns

**Wool Works**
www.woolworks.org/resources
Provides a fantastic list of resources and excellent links to other relevant sites.

**Yarndex**
www.yarndex.com
The Yarn Directory featuring over 5,000 different yarns.

**Yarn Harlot**
www.yarnharlot.ca
Knitting blog with excellent archive of information.

**Trend Forecasting Services**

For the latest fashion, design and trend information predicting colours, yarns, fabrics and style directions:

**Carlin International**
Head Office, 79 Rue de Miromesnil,
75008 Paris, France
Tel: + 33 (0) 1 53 04 42 00
Email: mcserin@carlin-groupe.com
www.carlin-international.com

**Committee for Colour and Trends**
60 Madison Avenue, Suite 1209,
New York 10010, USA
Tel: + 1 212 532 3555
Email: info@colourandtrends.com
www.colourandtrends.com

**Fashion Forecast Service**
302 New Street, Brighton, Victoria 3186, Australia
Email: info@fashionforecastservices.com
www.fashionforecastservices.com.au

**Mudpie Ltd**
21–24 Home Farm Business Centre, Lockerley,
Romsey, Hampshire, SO51 0JT, UK
Tel: + 44 20 3005 1000
Email: enquire@mudpie.co.uk
www.trendjournal.mudpie.co.uk

**Nelly Rodi**
28 Avenue de Saint-Ouen,
75018 Paris, France
Tel: + 44 (0)142 9304 06
Email: infos@nellyrodi.com
www.nellyrodi.com

**Peclers**
23 Rue du Mail, 75002 Paris, France
Tel : + 33 (0) 1 40 41 06 06
Email: peclers@peclersparis.com
www.peclersparis.com

**Promostyl**
Promostyl (Head Office)
5 Passage Thiere, 75011 Paris, France
www.promostyl.com

**Trendstop.com**
28–39 The Quadrant, 135 Salisbury Road,
London NW6 6RJ, UK
Tel: + 44 (0) 870 788 6888
www.trendstop.com

**Trends West**
6399 Wilshire Boulevard Suite 1000, Los Angeles,
California 90048, USA
Tel: + 1 323 622 2200
Email: info@trendswest.com
www.trendswest.com

**WGSN (Worth Global Style Network)**
Greater London House, Hampstead Road,
London NW1 7EJ, UK
Tel: + 44 (0)20 7728 4390
Email:sales@4C.wgsn.com.
www.wgsn.com

# FURTHER READING AND USEFUL RESOURCES

## Introduction

Christiansen, Betty, *Knitting For Peace: Make the World a Better Place One Stitch at a Time*. New York: Stewart, Tabori & Chang, 2006

Greer, Betsy, *Knitting for Good*. Massachusetts: Trumpeter Books, 2008

McFadden, David Revere; Scanlan, Jennifer & Steifle Edwards, Jennifer, *Radical Lace and Subversive Knitting*. New York: Museum of Modern Art and Design, 2007

Moor, Mandy & Prain, Leanne, *Yarn Bombing: The Art of Crochet and Knit Graffiti*. Vancouver: Arsenal Pulp Press, 2009

Turney, Joanne, *The Culture of Knitting*. Oxford: Berg, 2009

## Chapter 1 The Knitting Industry

Black, Sandy, *Knitwear for Fashion*. London: Thames & Hudson, 2005

Brackenbury, Terry, *Knitted Clothing Technology*. Oxford: Blackwell Scientific Publications, 1992

Brown, Carol, *Fashion and Textiles: The Essential Careers Guide*. London: Laurence King Publishing, 2010

Fogg, Marnie, *Vintage Fashion Knitwear: Collecting and Wearing Design Classics*. London: Carlton Books Ltd, 2010

Harvey, Michael, *Patons: A Story of Machine Knitting*. Berkshire: Springwood Books, 1985

Kiewe, Heinz Edgar, *History of Knitting: Is It Earlier than Weaving?* Oxford: Art Needlework Industries Ltd, 1976

Spencer, David J, *Knitting Technology: A Comprehensive Handbook and Practical Guide to Modern-Day Principles and Practices*, Cambridge: Woodhead Publishing Ltd; revised edition, 2001

## Chapter 2 Research and Design

Davies, Hywel, *Fashion Designers' Sketchbooks*. London: Laurence King Publishing, 2010

Donofrio-Ferrezza, Lisa & Hefferen, Marilyn, *Designing a Knitwear Collection*. New York: Fairchild Books, 2008

Martin, Raymond, *The Trend Forecaster's Handbook*. London: Laurence King Publishing, 2010

Smith, P, *You Can Find Inspiration in Everything (And If You Can't, Look Again)*. London: Thames & Hudson, 2003

Wesen Bryant, Michele, *Fashion Drawing: Illustration Techniques for Fashion Designers* Laurence King Publishing, 2011

## Chapter 3 Working with Colour and Texture

Allen, John, *Treasury of Machine-Knitted Stitches*, London: David & Charles, 1989

Boeger, Lexi, *Intertwined: The Art of Handspun Yarn, Modern Patterns and Creative Spinning* Massachusetts: Quarry Books, 2010

Christoffersson, Britt-Marie, *Pop Knitting: Bold Motifs Using Color & Stitch*. Colorado: Interweave Press Inc., 2012

Guagliumi, Susan, *Hand-Manipulated Stitches for Machine Knitters*. Charleston, South Carolina: BookSurge, 2008

Nabney, Janet, *An Illustrated Handbook of Machine Knitting*. London: BT Batsford Ltd, 1987

Scully, Kate & Johnston Cobb, Debra, *Colour Forecasting for Fashion*. London: Laurence King Publishing, 2012

Smith, Mary & Bunyan, Chris, *A Shetland Knitter's Notebook*. Shetland: The Shetland Times Ltd, 1991

Stanley, Montse, *Knitter's Handbook*. Devon: David & Charles, 1988

Thomas, Mary, *Knitting Book*. London: Hodder & Stoughton, 1938

Thomas, Mary, *Mary Thomas's Book of Knitting Patterns*. London: Hodder & Stoughton Ltd, 1943

## Chapter 4 Innovative Techniques

Bowles, M & Isaac, C, *Digital Textile Design*. London: Laurence King Publishing, 2009

Braddock Clarke, Sarah E & O'Mahony, Marie, *Techno Textiles 2: Revolutionary Fabrics for Fashion and Design*. London: Thames & Hudson, 2007

Brown, Sass, *Eco Fashion*. London: Laurence King Publishing, 2010

Lee, Ruth, *Contemporary Knitting for Textile Artists*. London: Batsford, 2007

Nabney, Janet, *Machine-knitted Fabrics: Felting Techniques*. London: BT Batsford Ltd, 1982

## Chapter 5 From Design to Production

Chunman Lo, Dennic, *Pattern Cutting*. London: Laurence King Publishing, 2011

Di Marco, Sally, *Draping Basics*. New York: Fairchild Books, 2010

Michelson, Carmen & Davis, Mary-Ann, *The Knitter's Guide to Sweater Design*. Colorado: Interweave Press, 1989

Nakamichi, Tomoko, *Pattern Magic: Stretch Fabrics*. London: Laurence King Publishing, 2012

Nakamichi, Tomoko, *Pattern Magic 2*. London: Laurence King Publishing, 2012

Szkutnicka, Basia, *Technical Drawing for Fashion*. London: Laurence King Publishing, 2010

Thompson, E, *Pressing Matters: Machine Knitter's Guide to Pressing and Finishing*. Birmingham: Erica Thompson Publication, 1991

# INDEX

**Page numbers in *italics* refer to illustrations**

# PICTURE CREDITS

Laurence King Publishing Ltd wish to thank the following institutions and individuals who have kindly provided photographic material for use in this book. While every effort has been made to trace the present copyright holders, we apologize in advance for any unintentional omission or error and will be pleased to insert the appropriate acknowledgement in any subsequent edition.

p4 Jennifer Chua (2011)
p6 Petronella Ytsma, Rania Hassan
p7 Peter Christian Christensen, Llot Lov
   www.llotlov.com, Bauke Knottnerus
p8 Alison Murray
p9 Linda Nellett, Corrine Bayraktaroglu
p10 Christopher Moore/Catwalking.com
p13 LatinContent/Getty Images
p15 Catwalking
p16 WHOLEGARMENT/Shima Seiki
p17 Christopher Moore/
   Catwalking, WireImage, WireImage
p18 Designkompagniet/Iben Høj
   www.ibenhoej.com
p19 Ginna Lee
p20 Ronald Siemoneit/Sygma/Corbis, Douglas
   Atfield/Castle Museum, Nottingham
p21 Nicola Bell www.inherglory.co.uk,
   Sabine Seymour
p22 Anne-Mette Manelius, Signe Emdal
p23 Signe Emdal, Courtesy of Beth Brown-
   Reinsel, Signe Emdal
p24 Courtesy of Beth Brown-Reinsel
p25 Signe Emdal
p26 Xenia Bluhum
p27 Jens Lindworsky
p28 Signe Emdal, Pitti Immagine Filati/Iafil/
   Francesco Guazzelli
p31 Pitti Immagine Filati/Accademia Italiana
   Filati/Francesco Guazzelli
p32–33 Hannah Risdon,Pitti Immagine Filati/
   Linea Piu/Francesco Guazzelli,Pitti Immagine
   Filati/Mille Fili/Francesco Guazzelli
p34 Ellis Scott email laura theiss
p36–37 Christopher Dadey
p38 Sundus Akhter
p40 Melanie Rickey Fashioneditoratlarge.com
p42 Amber Hards
p43 Fumiko Kozuka
p44–45 Elena Muñoz Gomez-Trenor
p46 Stelianour Sani, Gemma Darby
p47 Caroline Prince
p50–51 Rory Jack Longdon
p52–53 De Monfort University
p54–55 courtesy of SPINEXPO TM – SHANGHAI
   & NEW YORK
p56 Amy Komocki
p57 Rachael Hewson
p58 WireImage, Lauren Sanins
   www.laurensanins.com
p59 Christopher Moore at Catwalking.com
p61 © Etienne Tordoir/Catwalkpictures
p65 AFP/Getty Images
p67 Hannah Risdon
p69 Paw Ager, Peter Gehrke, David Shih/
   Monica YT Huang
p70 Paw Ager
p71 Randy Brooke

p72 Randy Brooke
p73 AFP/Getty Images
p74–75 Giuseppe Simone Bertolucci
p76 WireImage
p78 AFP/Getty Images
p79 Nikki Gabriel
p80 Lexi Boeger
p82 Stephen Jessop
p85 Gamma-Rapho/Getty Images,
p86 Gamma-Rapho/Getty Images, catwalking.com,
   Hannah Louise Buswell
p87 David Poole
p88 Genevieve Sweeney, Andy Espin, Etienjones,
   Roger Dean/Getty Images
p89 AFP/Getty Images, ACM Photography/
   Kevin Kramp
p92 Emma Gibney
p93 Philip Meech
p94 Randy Brooke
p95 Astrid Cordier, Elana Adler
p97 Bella Howard
p98 Nikki Gabriel
p99 Sophie Dreijer, Anne Sofie Madsen
p101 Hannah Risdon
p103 Jade Drew,WireImage
p104 Catwalking.com
p105 Catwalking.com
p106 Getty Images for Michael Kors
p110 Hannah Rachel Simpson
p111 Boy Kortekaas
p112 AFP/Getty Images, Carmen Leng
p113 Thomas Klementsson
p114 Catwalking.com
p115 AFP/Getty Images, Catwalking.com
p116–117 Designkompagniet/Iben Høj
   www.ibenhoej.com
p121 Jazmine Rocks/Elizabeth Dyson
p122 Jazmine Rocks/Helena Rees
p123 Hanjoo Kim
p124 Getty Images
p125 Hannah Risdon
p126 Sue Bradley
p127 Dora Kelemen
p128 Catwalking.com
p129 WireImage, Jenny Postle
p130 HJSwainson, Florence Spurling
p131 Lauren Fenn
p133 Rosalind Price-Cousins
p134 Roel Van Tour
p136–137 Kenzie Burchell and Jez Tozier,
   Christien Meindertsma
p138 Mei-En Lien, Johan Ku
p140 Rene Habermacher
p141 Peter Gehrke, Thomas Klementsson
p142 Kim Choong Wilkins
p143 Callum Aldrin Smith, Adrian Wilson
p144–145 Seung Rok Baek
p146 Elana Adler
p147 Catwalking.com
p148 Tamás Réthey-Prikkel
p149 Jens Lindworosky
p150 Alison Waite
p151 Dan Gardner
p152 Uli Weber
p153 Uli Weber, Robert Rowland
p154-155 Karen Philippi
p156 Sundus Akhter, Ralph Emerson
p157 Amy Hunt
p158 Johan Ku
p159 Ginna Lee
p160 Zoe HItchen
p161 Craig Lawrence

p162 Daniel Jolly
p163 Kevin Muth, Makepiece www.makepiece.co.uk
p164–165 Merel Karhof
p166 Rafael Krötz Fotografie/Rafael Krötz for Stoll
p167 Na'ama Rietti
p170 Na'ama Rietti
p171 Marcela Abal and Maria Ines Paysse
p172 Alexandra Aldridge
   www.alexandraaldridge.com
p176 Samuel Bailey
p177 Christopher Dadey
p181 Alexandra Aldridge
   www.alexandraaldridge.com
p182 Beatrice Korlekie Newman
p191 (top) dm909/Getty Images;
   (bottom) © Tom Bean/Corbis
p196 Alexandra Aldridge
   www.alexandraaldridge.com,
   Beatrice Korlekie Newman
p197 Alexandra Aldridge
   www.alexandraaldridge.com
p198 Alexandra Aldridge
   www.alexandraaldridge.com

# ACKNOWLEDGEMENTS

I would like to thank everyone who has supported this project. In particular I would like to thank Sandra Backlund, Mark Fast, Iben Høj, Craig Lawrence, Derek Lawlor, Alessandra Marchi, Issey Miyake, Beatrice Korlekie Newman, Alice Palmer, Veronika Persché and Brooke Roberts.

I am also grateful to the many companies and associations who have given their support to this project and who have offered advice and guidance, particularly Texere Yarns Ltd, who have sponsored many of the stunning yarns featured in this book and to Joanne Smith, Director of Texere Yarns, for her interest in the project; to De Montfort University; Emdal Colorknit; Gerald Alt at 'I Knit London'; Knitone; Llot Llov; Makepiece; Patons and Baldwin's; Pringle of Scotland; Shima Seika Ltd; SPINEXPO; H. Stoll GmbH & Co; Textprint and University of Northampton.
In addition, grateful thanks go to the following people:
Marcela Abal; Elana Adler; Sundus Akhter; Alexandra Aldridge; Lexi Boeger; Sue Bradley; Sarah Burton; Hannah Louise Buswell; Shao Yen Chen; Kim Choong Wilkins; Alana Clifton-Cunningham; Cooperative Designs; Gemma Darby; Jade Drew; Yang Du; Elizabeth Dyson; Electronic Sheep; Signe Emdal; Lauren Fenn; Rania Hassan; Nikki Gabriel; the Jafagirls (Corrine Bayraktaroglu and Nancy Mellon); Amber Hards; Rachel Hewson; Amy Hunt; Maria Ines Paysse; Merel Karhof; Katwise; Dora Keleman; Hanjoo Kim; Bauke Knottnerus; Amy Komocki; Fumiko Kozuka; Kevin Kramp; Johan Ku; Stine Ladefoged; Gina Lee; Rory Jack Longdon; Angela McBride; Anne Sofie Madsen; Jessica Medlock; Christina Meindertsma; Elena Muñoz Gomez-Trenor; Alison Murray; Linda Nellet; Marina Nikolaeva; Laduma Ngxokolo; Claire-Ann O'Brien; Jeung-Hwa Park; Rosalind Price-Cousins; Jenny Postle; Steven Oo; Popska; Caroline Prince; Helena Rees; Melanie Rickey; Na'ama Rietti; Hannah Risdon; Freddie Robins; Lauren Sanins; Karen Searle; Irina Shaposhnikova; Laura Siegal; Florence Spurling; Genevieve Sweeney; Laura Theiss; Nicky Thomson; Claire Tough; Alison Waite; Stacey Wettstein.

A special thank you goes to Anne Townley, my Development Editor, for all her kindness, continuing encouragement, patience and support in the planning and preparation of the book, as well as to Helen Rochester, Commissioning Editor; Peter Jones, Senior Editor, and to all involved with this book at Laurence King Publishing. I would also like to acknowledge the support of Annalaura Palma, the picture researcher, for her continued enthusiasm throughout the project, and Matthew Andrew, Dave Overton and Kalina Krawczyk for their dedication in photographing many of the samples.

In addition I would like to say a huge thank you to all my friends and colleagues at University Campus Suffolk and to previous colleagues for their enthusiastic support throughout this project, particularly Tricia Clark, Polly Lancaster and Marie-Thérèse Pumfrey.

On a personal note I would like to say a huge thank you to Chloe Sage; Catherine Burge and Sol Burge for their encouragement and support, and the copious meetings and coffee; to all my family and friends for their patience; and most of all my parents George and Margaret Brown for their brilliant support, continuous encouragement and belief in all that I do. This book is dedicated to them.